Wayne H. Tyler

Women
in a
Changing World

EDITED BY UTA WEST

New York   St. Louis   San Francisco   Düsseldorf   Mexico   Montreal
Panama   São Paulo   Toronto   New Delhi   Kuala Lumpur   London
Rio de Janeiro   Sydney   Singapore   Johannesburg

McGraw-Hill Book Company

Book design by Paulette Nenner

23456789MUMU79876

Library of Congress Cataloging in Publication Data

Main entry under title:

Women in a changing world.

     CONTENTS: Piercy, M. Rough times.—West, U. Introduction.—Janeway, E. The weak are the second sex. [etc.]
     1. Feminism—Addresses, essays, lectures.
I. West, Uta.
HQ1154.W883   301.41'2   75-22278
ISBN 0-07-069465-6

The Authors

Donald Barthelme was born in Philadelphia, raised in Texas, and has lived in New York City for the past fifteen years. He is the author of *Snow White,* a novel, and three collections of short stories: *City Life, Sadness, Guilty Pleasures.* His fiction has appeared in *The New Yorker, The Atlantic Monthly,* and *Harper's,* among others.

Mary Daly is the author of *The Church and the Second Sex* and *Beyond God the Father.* She holds doctorates in theology and philosophy from the University of Fribourg, Switzerland, and is currently associate professor of theology at Boston College, where she teaches courses in feminist studies. She has published many scholarly articles and lectured widely on women's liberation.

Lois Gould lives in New York City, is married to a psychiatrist, and has two children. She has published three novels: *Such Good Friends, Necessary Objects,* and *Final Analysis,* as well as books of nonfiction, stories, and articles which have appeared in such publications as *The New York Times, Ms., New York* Magazine, and *McCall's.*

Barbara Grizzuti Harrison is a widely published freelance writer whose work appears regularly in such periodicals as *New Republic, Ms., McCall's, Esquire,* and *New York* Magazine. She lives in New York with her two children, a boy of eleven and a girl of twelve.

Elizabeth Janeway is a novelist, journalist, critic, and lecturer. A graduate of Barnard, she published six novels between 1953 and 1964. Her widely acclaimed first nonfiction book, *Man's World, Woman's Place,* was published in 1971. This was followed in 1975 by *Between Myth and Morning: Women Awakening.* Ms. Janeway lives in New York City with her husband. She is active in a number of professional organizations such as P.E.N. and The Authors Guild.

Jane Lazarre lives in Manhattan, holds a master's degree in anthropology, and has taught English literature in New York City high schools. She was a student in training at the American Institute for Psychotherapy and Psychoanalysis. Ms. Lazarre is married and has two children.

Doris Lessing was born of British parents in Persia, grew up in Southern Rhodesia, and settled in England in 1949. A distinguished author of novels, stories, reportage, poems, and plays, too numerous to be listed here, she achieved worldwide recognition with the publication in 1962 of *The Golden Notebook,* which remains a milestone in feminist writings.

Anaïs Nin was born in Paris and educated in the United States. She returned to Paris, where she wrote her first novels, and remained there until the outbreak of World War II. When American publishers refused her work, she bought a printing press and published her own books. With the appearance of her multi-volumed *Diary,* Ms. Nin's work gained great popularity, especially among young people. She received the honorary degree of Doctor of Fine Arts from the Philadelphia College of Fine Arts, and in 1974 she was elected to the National Institute of Arts and Letters. Ms. Nin divides her time between her New York and California residences.

Grace Paley was born and educated in New York City, where she still lives. She has two children. She has taught at Columbia University and Sarah Lawrence College. *New American Review, Esquire,* and *Atlantic,* among others, have published Ms. Paley's fiction. In 1961, she won a Guggenheim fellowship in fiction. She is the author of a collection of short stories, *The Little Disturbances of Man,* published in 1956, and *Enormous Changes at the Last Minute,* her most recent short story collection, which appeared in 1975.

Marge Piercy, poet and novelist, has been active in the women's liberation movement since 1967. Her first novel, *Going Down Fast,* was published in 1969, followed by *Dance the Eagle to Sleep* in 1970, and *Small Changes* in 1973. She is the author of three books of poems: *Breaking Camp,* published in 1968, *Hard Loving* in 1970, and *To Be of Use* in 1973. Ms. Piercy has read her poetry throughout the country and has lectured widely on feminism. Born in Detroit, she now lives on Cape Cod.

Caryl Rivers, author and journalist, is an associate professor of Public Communications at Boston University, where she teaches writing. She is also media critic for the *Boston Globe.* Born near Washington, D.C., Ms. Rivers was educated at Trinity College and Columbia University's graduate School of Journalism. She is the author of *Aphrodite at Mid-Century,* and her articles have appeared in *The New York Times, The Saturday Review, Ms., The Nation,* and *Rolling Stone.* Ms. Rivers is married and has two children.

Michael Weiss grew up in New York City and now lives in San Francisco. He graduated from Knox College and received a master's degree from Johns Hopkins University. He has worked as a reporter for the *Baltimore News American* and the *Baltimore Sun,* taught at Temple University and the University of California at Berkeley. Mr. Weiss is the author of a book on a year in the life of a city commune, called *Living Together.* The article reprinted here is based on his experiences in that nine-person Philadelphia commune.

Uta West grew up in New York City, received her B.A. from Brooklyn College, and did graduate work at Columbia University. She has taught at Denver University and the College of the Virgin Islands. Ms. West has written three novels, and her articles have appeared in *Viva, Penthouse, Countdown,* and *Pageant.* The selection included here is part of a book in progress which deals with contemporary relationships. Ms. West lives on Cape Cod with her ten-year-old daughter.

Contents

Acknowledgment

I would like to thank my editor, James Wallace, for the inspiration and support that made this book possible.

Thanks are due, also, to Karyn Martin, for her help and cooperation.

Uta West
INTRODUCTION

The spirit of the Sober Seventies seems to require that we take a long, hard look at the revolutionary ferment of the past decades and how it has affected our lives. During the Soaring Sixties, too much seemed to be happening too fast; in sad-but-wiser retrospect it often appears that not enough *real* changes took place, and that all that sound and fury signified very little. This pessimistic view has more to do with disappointed hopes than with realistic evaluations, however. It merely indicates that the changes which *did* occur were not to our liking, and thus were either dismissed or else went unrecognized. The women's liberation movement has, so far, largely avoided this kind of public stocktaking, subordinating it to the more urgent political necessity of presenting a united front. But now, it seems, the need to sort things out, to separate the wheat from the chaff, can no longer be postponed. For we may have come a long way, as the advertisement unctuously assures us, but most of us are more interested in where we are now; and we are uncertain of where we have come *to,* let alone where we might be going. From those who say we haven't gone far enough, to those who cry that we've gone too far already and in the wrong direction, nobody seems really satisfied with the situation of women today.

While there is little room for complacency, there is less reason for despair—for the kind of apathy or reactionary "nostalgia" which currently afflicts many people, especially the young, and which is merely the reverse of the starry-eyed idealism of a few years back. The very profusion of views, this ongoing questioning and exploring, is a sure sign that the women's movement is alive and well—that, like any living, growing thing, it refuses to be boxed and labeled, but continues obstinately to overflow the boundaries we try to set for it.

Confusion and contradiction are part of the process of evolution Mary Daly has called "the becoming of women." It means learning that liberation cannot be achieved in a single bounding leap, or even a series of them, and that no amount of ideology is a substitute for unremitting, day-to-day awareness.

"What is happening to women," says Elizabeth Janeway, "involves a sudden enlargement of our world; the sky above us lifts, light pours in. Certainly that illumination reveals fear, anger, frustration, doubt, uncertainty. . . . No maps exist for this enlarged world, we must make them as we explore. . . ."

That the freedom trail is rocky and torturous, full of pain, bewilderment and terror, should have come as no surprise to women. After all, no one *really* promised us a rose garden. But the early explorers, understandably, tended to stress the positive aspects of the liberation adventure—not just the rightness and necessity of it, but the excitement, the exhilaration. Anger was an energizer, a catalyst for action, and a certain amount of oversimplification was necessary, at the beginning, to spur us on and give us the courage to break the molds. We can hardly blame the Mss. Friedan, Millet, Greer, and Steinem for not warning us of all the pitfalls and boobytraps they couldn't possibly foresee. Like any pioneers, they could only indicate certain guidelines which (as many women soon came to realize) could not be followed too rigidly. It may be just as well that the women's revolution has no real leaders (turned into superstars by the media, these above-mentioned women were forced to defend their positions rather than continue their explorations, and thus they lost much of their credibility). However we go about our struggle for full humanity, we will have to take into account the particular circumstances of our lives, the needs and limitations of our individual personalities.

This book, then, might be viewed as a report from the unsung infantry of the liberation, the many women and fewer men who have ventured upon new paths, sometimes by choice, more often from necessity—because changes in the world forced them to revise the way they thought and lived. If this collection tends to be personal rather than political, this emphasis corresponds to the priorities of our lives, as we

---

perceive them; the hunger in our bellies is more urgent than the famine in the land, and one who is miserable emotionally may have little energy or inclination for tackling the problems of the globe.

Much of our difficulty revolves around the inevitable gap between our ideals and the boundaries reality sets upon what is possible at any given point in time and space. Our firmest convictions and best intentions have a way of crashing head-long into the walls of our fears and desires. When old patterns refuse to disappear simply because they are no longer wanted, we become discouraged; we are tempted to despair. We did not quite understand, as we crawled out of the slime and stood upright, breathing the cold, sharp air, just how tough it was going to be. The answer to Freud's classic question, "What do women really want?" is *everything!*—the securities and comforts of the old, plus all the rights and benefits of the new. Sure, we are asking too much, but it is only natural. In the past we were content to ask for far too little.

"Women," says Mary Daly, "are struggling with the tensions between remembrance of the past and experience of the present, which contradicts our old beliefs." To this we must add a third factor—our hopes and aspirations for the future, which also tend to be negated by the realities of our daily lives. In this triple bind, we may be hard put to find "the enemy." Women's liberation is no exception to the rule that it is easier to blame "the other" (in this case, men) for all our difficulties and shortcomings. But blaming others will not help us now, for we are all in this together, women and men and children, and even animals; our very lives depend on fighting "the system," and the majority of men, whether they are aware of it or not, are as victimized as we are by the forces of sexism and patriarchy.

It is hard to accept the fact that in our personal confrontations with impersonal evil, ideology is only of limited help. The struggles of a lifetime cannot be reduced to political dogma without seriously distorting experience and banalizing our profoundest inner feelings, thus preventing us from seeing things as they are, not as we think they *should* be. Rather than recognize the inherent limits of all ideologies, we expect them

Women in a Changing World

to vouchsafe our personal salvation, and if they fail to do so, we feel betrayed. It is this feeling which accounts for the current success of writers like Midge Decter *(The Liberated Woman and Other Americans; The New Chastity)*, Arianna Stassinopoulos *(The Female Woman)*, and George Gilder *(Sexual Suicide; Naked Nomads)*. One cannot entirely dismiss these "backlash" defectors, for they appeal to the many women (and men) who are bewildered by the rhetoric and disappointed by the promises of the women's movement, and thus are easily seduced by the questionable contention that, since the ideals of liberation aren't really "working," there must be something wrong with the ideals themselves. Running through the scholarly research, the welter of statistics, the well-wrought arguments and well-turned phrases of these writers is the frightened reactionary soul crying: "Look what you've done, look at the mess you're making of people's lives!"

It is true that the battlefields of liberation are strewn with wreckage—with broken dreams and hearts, with shattered hopes and illusions. But there is really no question of turning back. Once you have taken that first step, once your eyes have been opened, the way to the past is barred forever. It makes no difference whether or not this first step is taken voluntarily. More and more, it is the traditional pattern that rejects the woman, rather than the other way around. For instance, should a woman find herself widowed, or divorced, her economic and social standing will change, whether she wants it to or not. As Elizabeth Janeway points out in the essay which opens this book, "The Weak Are the Second Sex," most women are in the labor force from brute economic necessity, and the more than six million single-mother heads-of-households have hardly any choice in the matter. Speculations as to what women should and should not do have little relevance to the reality of our lives, which is that we have been hurled out there to cope with the future-shock changes of a world we never made and don't really understand.

Ms. Janeway shows us that the revolution has already *happened*, and is continuing to happen quite apart from us, the result of social, economic, and political forces that have been operative for some time. The strength of the women's movement lies in the fact that it is a *response to,* rather than a cause of, current upheavals in values and lifestyles. Revolutions involve so much chaos and destruction that they tend to occur only as a last resort—when the old bargains between the haves and have-nots of power can no longer be made viable. The question of power is at the heart of the passionate, irrational resistance to women's liberation by men whose only claim to superiority is membership in that dubious fraternity known as "man's world." Now that even this tenuous claim is threatened, the majority of men are being forced to examine their own questionable relationship to the power structure, and they are understandably loath to accept the fact that it is the powerless, rather than women as such, who constitute the second sex.

There is also passionate resistance on the part of men who feel their very survival depends on the function of women as magnifying mirrors that reflect men at twice their actual size. Such men make women the keepers of virtues like compassion, humility, patience, and forbearance, which they themselves find impractical and impossible to live up to. Few men have written honestly about how the women's movement has affected them, and for this reason, if for no other, the writings of George Gilder merit attention. It is his contention that women inspire and "civilize" men, who without the motivation of marriage and family turn into barbarians and "naked nomads." But Mr. Gilder should not wonder why women are overturning his pedestal. By his own statistically proven admission, single women fare better than single men *or* married women, economically and psychologically. Obviously, men will have to cease their consuming dependence on women, which drains and diminishes us, and become psychically whole themselves. If, like Count Dracula, men can only live by feeding on women, it does not follow that we must acquiesce in the sacrifice.

It is useless to think, says Ms. Janeway, that men who have such high psychological stakes in the *status quo* will be persuaded by reasoned argument; most of them know, on the rational level, that our cause is just, and will pay lip service to such principles as equal pay for equal work. But it is equally unrealistic to think we can accomplish our aims all by ourselves through separatism of a kind. According to Ms. Janeway, the women's movement is still largely talking to itself.

Mythologies do change when they no longer fit our social needs. They have already begun to change. In the meantime, during this period of transition, it is important that we understand very clearly the nature of the forces we are up against. Unless we relate our goals and methods to these realities, we will be living in a fantasy world and talking to ourselves. Despite all the difficulties, Ms. Janeway sees no evidence that women are generally unhappy; on the contrary, she finds them "overwhelmingly energetic, cheerful, funny and good-natured," as they go about the business of getting on with life.

While getting on with it, we may need to pause now and then to survey the terrain, and to determine from which angle we may best continue our journey. In the essay called "God Is a Verb," Mary Daly offers us the panoramic view, the breadth of perspective we need to persevere through the disappointments and setbacks we are bound to suffer, as we pursue our limited objectives. According to Ms. Daly, the women's revolution is essentially a spiritual one, for it is woman who must totally redefine and charge with new life the old concepts of transcendent reality. When we have gone beyond God the Father, we may begin to understand the true nature of "the search for ultimate meaning and reality, which some would call God."

Ms. Daly helps us to see that our problems stem not from having set our sights too high, but on the contrary, from being willing to settle for too many half-measures and compromises. Reforms within the patriarchal structure are ultimately useless, and the goal of achieving equality with men is essentially a self-destructive one for women, since it perpetuates a system of values that must be wholeheartedly rejected and destroyed if we are to become whole and free, androgynous human beings.

This concept of androgyny is carried even further by Andrea Dworkin, who, in her book *Woman-Hating,* advocates nothing short of the complete abolition of the family as we know it in favor of a more tribal way of life, with removal of most sexual taboos, including those of incest. While such a utopia may remain out of sight and reach for most of us, it is significant that there are those among us who glimpse the farther shores. Ms. Dworkin's prophetic vision can serve as inspiration to those who believe, and dare to follow that distant star, while Ms. Daly offers hope and consolation to the many women who didn't know what to do with their strong, and seemingly anachronistic, religious feelings. Ms. Daly's revolutionary views are based on solid philosophical and theological ground, on thorough scholarship as well as a deep insight into the human condition. She helps us to understand that sexism is the original model for every form of racism, of "we" against "the other," and that this will not change as long as human traits continue to be arbitrarily divided into masculine and feminine. An Arianna Stassinopoulos, who glories in the differences between the sexes, which she insists are innate, and sees no reason why "separate but equal" should not work out fine for everybody, is being naïve and simpleminded in the extreme, and doing women a great disservice by promising us that we can have our cake and eat it too. Ms. Stassinopoulos takes issue, point by point, with the feminist manifestoes of Kate Millet and Germaine Greer (*Sexual Politics* and *The Female Eunuch*), but the distinction she insists on—between liberation and emancipation—is only semantic and ideological nit-picking, the sort of infighting that ignores all the larger questions of politics, economics, and history, of psychology and religion, which determine the kind of equality and justice women can expect.

Just as we cannot take the concept of equality at face value, so it is important to realize that permission is not at all the same as freedom, which, being an inner condition, can therefore not be *given* to anybody. Her failure to make this distinction renders specious the arguments of Midge Decter, who asserts that American women already have more freedom than they know what to do with, more options, according to Ms. Decter, than are good and healthy for us, so that we refuse to accept the limitations and obligations of becoming adults. But it does not take much perception to see that most of the bewildering array of choices offered to us are illusory. Choosing among unreal, unworkable alternatives is *not* freedom. If women still want to marry and have children, this does not necessarily express their "true" nature, for the truth of that nature, or even its existence as something apart, is a matter for debate. It simply means that the Brave-New-World programs we've been offered are still largely based on masculine models—the only ones we really know—and do not reflect the real needs of women. One such program is the new sexual permissiveness, a theme that engages the respective reportorial skills of Barbara Harrison and Lois Gould, who in their different ways examine the difficulties women have conforming to current ideas of how we ought to behave. Whether the permission comes from the sexual revolutionaries or the radical feminists, "you may" has a way of sounding an awful lot like "you must." If Margaret Mead, no less, tells us it's okay to be bisexual, and Masters and Johnson urge us on to multiple orgasms, what exactly does this mean? You may be doing it more and enjoying it less; or if you're *not* doing it, you may be worried about *that*, thinking: What's wrong with me, I don't really feel like going to bed with other women, and porn films leave me cold! If this is your problem, take heart: you are not alone!

In "Sexual Chic, Sexual Fascism, and Sexual Confusion," Ms. Harrison finds that woman plus woman adds up to as much perplexity, anxiety, and frustration as woman plus man. In part this is true because many women are having sex with each other not out of any genuine inclination, but out of some head- rather than gut-oriented conviction that this is the correct or with-it thing to do. In talking to women who are experimenting with lesbianism and bisexuality, Ms. Harrison discovered that experiences and responses differed widely, but that we tend to bring our hangups, our old preconceptions and expectations into the new relationships. In lesbian society as elsewhere you will find "role-playing straight out of Central Casting," as one woman put it. In any case, Ms. Harrison found it impossible to classify or draw any conclusions about women on the basis of whom they chose as bedpartners.

Lois Gould studies the new "Pornography for Women" and finds few takers. Offered entree into this hitherto all-male world, women discover little there to hold their interest. Porn filmmakers, eager to attract the money of female customers, may soften the core a bit, but they are still dishing up the old classic male fantasy, which depicts woman either as willing slave-victim or else as whore-priestess and whip mistress. The basic premise, according to Ms. Gould, remains: dominate or be dominated. What turns on the majority of women, as well as more sophisticated men, whose sexual consciousness has been raised above the average, is the total spectrum of the sexual interchange—the rich, subtle, complex emotional, psychological, and physical factors involved in even the simplest couplings. The sexual equality that is being foisted upon us (on pain of being called inhibited and unliberated should we reject it) is nothing but the traditional male dream of impersonal, genitally oriented sex. Such "equality" prevents women from exploring the full dimensions of our own erotic needs and wishes.

These erotic dimensions *are* being explored, not by pornographers, but by women like Betty Dodson, an artist turned sex educator and therapist. Ms. Dodson conducts masturbation workshops for women, has shown her film on closed-circuit TV, and has written and illustrated a booklet, "Liberating Masturbation," wherein she tackles this hitherto unmentionable subject with candor, courage, and an almost missionary zeal. Women have described Ms. Dodson's approach as "refreshing," and she is reported to have had considerable success in redeeming masturbation from secrecy, guilt, and shame and in freeing women from the fear and loathing of their bodies. But Ms. Dodson's work suffers from the quantitative, mechanistic bias of the sexual-revolution schools, which feminists have justly rejected. It does not necessarily follow that a woman who possesses the skill and the freedom to pleasure herself to the fullest will be more successful in her sexual relation with others, for there is this essential difference: when you masturbate, you are totally *in control,* as you can not and must not be with a partner. Bigger and better orgasms, or even transcendental ones, are no guarantee that the woman (or the man) will find the sexual experience psychologically satisfying. In masturbation there is an essential ingredient missing, namely the human connection involved (as one woman expressed it: "Nothing to touch but your own body").

This complicated human connection is the theme of the selection called "If Love Is the Answer, What Is the Question?" A great deal of conflict revolves around the ideals of romantic love, which many of us have come to reject, intellectually and practically, but which nevertheless continue to have a powerful hold on our psyches. As old values and patterns disintegrate, the ensuing uncertainty only reinforces the deep-seated human need for some kind of pair-bonding, which may seem more than ever the only bulwark against loneliness and alienation. As the title suggests, there is no simple solution; there is only the necessity of coming to terms with pain and paradox.

Sometimes difficulties may seem overwhelming because we are in the midst of them; we cannot see the forest for the trees and need to attain some distance before we can evaluate the situation as a whole. In her essay "In Favor of the Sensitive Man," Anaïs Nin looks at young couples from the perspective of nearly five decades of observing man-woman relationships, and on the whole she finds what she sees heartening. More and more, the young people she has come to know, as teacher and advisor, are abandoning old roles and relating to each other as equals and partners. This hopeful development is contingent upon the emergence of the "new man," whom Ms. Nin sees as the proper mate and companion to the new woman. There is a problem, however, in the fact that gentleness and sensitivity are often taken for weakness in our culture, by women as well as men. It is yet another example of old and new values clashing head on: while abhorring the *macho*, women tend to admire the qualities of aggression and assertion (perhaps because they have been so long denied us) and often have trouble accepting and respecting the totally unchauvinist male. He seems to be lacking something, some idea we may have of what constitutes virility; he does not fit our cherished impossible dream of the Ideal Man, who is both warrior and poet, boxer and violinist—hero of a thousand films, ever ferocious with his enemies, ever kind and considerate to his women. The sensitive man needs all the support and encouragement he can get, says Ms. Nin, and we cannot give it to him while hanging on to outmoded prejudices and predilections.

In "Diary of a Mad Househusband," one of these sensitive men, Michael Weiss, offers us an interesting insight: the monotony and compulsive quality of the endless household chores can serve as a tranquilizer and an escape—an excuse for failing to get on with one's life and work. Quite often the enslavement is largely self-imposed; the subtle brainwashing effect of housework may seem preferable to struggling with writer's block, for instance. To dissolve the block you have to stay with it—pace the floor, sharpen pencils, or whatever; but instead this homebound writer washes the dishes, mops the floor, or feeds the children to get rid of the unused energy and so the day won't count for a total loss. As Mr. Weiss realizes, the conditioning of women offers ample social and moral justification for taking this "easy" way out.

"The Bill," Donald Barthelme's short, deft jab at contemporary liaisons, shows us how a (sensitive?) man feels at the end of the affair. He feels "ripped off"—or maybe the word is exploited—and carries this feeling to its logical and literal conclusion, with results that are as hilarious as they are deadly. The two contributions to this book by men are brief, personal, and tongue-in-cheek; one might be tempted to draw the conclusion that men deal with interpersonal difficulties more humorously or flippantly than women do, but the jaundiced eye and satiric wit also inform Grace Paley's story "The Used-Boy Raisers," which explores the vicissitudes of that love- and lifestyle known as serial monogamy. Between the current husband and the former one, there does not seem much to choose (reminding me of the thrice-married woman who said, "For all the difference it made, I might as well still be with the first one"). The children too have some difficulty distinguishing between and finding the right stance to take with these "fathers." The constant in the lives of these "used-boys" is the mother, who describes her destiny as being "laughingly the servant of man."

The Paley woman's understanding of her situation contrasts ironically with her "feminine" behavior, which remains for the most part conciliatory. By contrast, the characters in Doris Lessing's "Not a Very Nice Story" think conventionally but behave otherwise. Unwitting pioneers, Ms. Lessing's nice, ordinary people become caught up in an extraordinary situation, much the way most of us do—because one thing simply led to another, and because, when confronted with a blatant contradiction between our moral values and our behavior, we simply put the blinders on. The determination "not to think about it" protects us against realizations that would have too devastating an effect upon our lives, and permits us to live with the irrational, the totally unacceptable; as such, this "blindness" may actually partake of some kind of higher wisdom. Ms. Lessing shows us, in her gently mocking, understated way, how our lives so often turn out quite other than we had any reason to expect.

For we cling to the belief that we are masters of our destiny and that whatever is wrong with our lives must be our own fault. This conviction reinforces what Caryl Rivers called "The New Anxiety of Motherhood." Faced with what may seem the most consequential decision of her life, a woman today must find her way among conflicting imperatives. Ms. Rivers details the bewilderment and distress of women faced with the bedrock, life-or-death question of motherhood, which perhaps more than any other epitomizes the existential dilemma of being a woman. The subjective ramifications of this subject go far beyond what has been said, either by the anti-baby contingent, which represents the predominant feminist view (or at least the one receiving the most publicity) and which considers children a personal and ecological liability, or by the glorifiers of Earth Mother, who view childbirth as a possibly political act. Caught in the middle, the ordinary woman who elects ordinary motherhood may find her problems ignored, or else treated with contempt.

Motherhood is also a concern for Jane Lazarre, who, in "What Feminists and Freudians Can Learn from Each Other," introduces the relatively new psychological concept of the "good enough" mother who, though flawed and imperfect, does not necessarily blight her children's lives. Other humans are allowed their imperfections, but mothers have had to carry a heavy burden of guilt, since they are held accountable for their children's psychic health. Ms. Lazarre explains how, once the gates of the unconscious are opened and we begin to explore the interior landscape, there is no telling *where* it might lead. In her case, as also in mine, a more or less classical psychoanalysis led, in the end, to feminism—an outcome that was not foreseen, and certainly not approved, by our respective therapists. But that's how things often happen, in real life, in the changing world, and more and more psychotherapists are becoming aware of this fact. As a result, the psychoanalytic establishment has begun to revise its theories and methods. Ms. Lazarre also reports on one of the most hopeful developments of recent years, the new feminist-oriented psychotherapy.

Unlike other critics of orthodox feminism, writers like Caryl Rivers, Mary Daly, and Jane Lazarre are engaged in what might be described as salvaging jobs, offering us not a choice between this or that, but the healing, enriching possibility of this *and* that. While Ms. Rivers tries, not all that figuratively, to save the baby from the dirty bathwater, and Ms. Daly allows us to accept our longing for, and experience of, transcendence, Ms. Lazarre shows us how to reconcile two powerful forces which can really help the growth of women. Though we are aware of the outrages perpetrated upon us in the name of God the Father, or Freud the Father, who commanded us to "Be fruitful and multiply," many women have nevertheless felt uneasy about the rejection by women's liberation of religion, psychotherapy, and motherhood. The nagging question remained: was it *all* a hoax, from beginning to end? And if so, what of the evidence of our experience—the moments of that peace which passeth understanding, the flashes of insight vouchsafed in our therapies, the joy of suckling a tiny infant?

If we need not deny these aspects of ourselves, we can, perhaps, live through this difficult period more easily. The mutants Marge Piercy talks about in her poem "Rough Times" must surely return now and then for a quick dip in the life-giving waters. The old Chinese curse, "May you live in interesting times," applies only to those who equate happiness with being placid and contented. Besides, happiness is not necessarily the ultimate value. There is an energy that inheres in our growing pains; when you expand, it produces a heightened sense of life, a quickening that makes pleasure and pain seem irrelevant—or rather, relevant only insofar as we are instructed by them, and pain seems to be by far the better teacher. True, not everyone is cut out to be an adventurer and explorer and one may well sympathize with the seasick woman who pleaded with the captain to stop the ship, if only for a few minutes. But we'll never get out of this world alive, and we may as well learn how to ride with the tide.

For those of us who understand the dangers and the hardships, as well as the pride and the glory of the unprecedented adventure known as the women's movement, stumbling and falling and going around in circles is part of the trip. There is nothing to do but pick ourselves up, dust ourselves off, and move on, perhaps marking the hidden rock, the unsuspected trap, so that others may be warned should they venture upon the same paths. Whether we opt for group marriage, serial monogamy, single motherhood, non-motherhood, bisexuality, promiscuity, the new psychotherapy, or the new spirituality, it would seem from the evidence that there are no magic formulas and no instant cures, and that the things we learn and experience differ considerably from what we've been promised or been told to fear. As antidotes to despair, there is nothing like a little hollow laughter, and the fierce kind of joy that comes from knowing that hope need not be squelched by disappointment, and that whatever doesn't destroy us makes us stronger.

Women in a Changing World

Marge Piercy
ROUGH TIMES

We are trying to live
as if we were an experiment
conducted by the future,

blasting cell walls
that no protective seal or inhibition
has evolved to replace.

I am conducting a slow vivisection
on my own tissues, carried out
under the barking muzzle of guns.

Those who speak of good and simple
in the same sandwich of tongue and teeth
inhabit some other universe.

Good draws blood from my scalp and files my nerves.
Good runs the yard engine of the night over my bed.
Good pickles me in the brown vinegar of guilt.
Good robs the easy words as they rattle off my teeth,
leaving me naked as an egg.

Remember that pregnancy is beautiful only
at a distance from the distended belly.
A new idea rarely is born like Venus attended by graces.
More commonly it's modeled of baling wire and acne.
More commonly it wheezes and tips over.

Most mutants die: only
a minority refract the race
through the prisms of their genes.

Those slimy fish with air sacs were ugly
as they hauled up on the mud flats
heaving and gasping. How clumsy we are
in this new air we reach with such effort
and can not yet breathe.

Marge Piercy
from LIVING IN THE OPEN

Elizabeth Janeway
THE WEAK ARE THE SECOND SEX

The women's liberation movement—Am I boring you already? Do the words turn you off? Then hang on for a minute, because that's what I want to talk about: the current state of mind which doesn't quite oppose ''women's lib'' but would really rather not hear any more about it at this point in time. It is very like the Silent Majority's reaction to Watergate-and-all-that: something has obviously been going on that should not have been, we admit that. But now we've admitted it (Yes, women should be paid equal wages for equal work. Yes, the President ought to give up the tapes), why don't you go away and stop bothering us?

This is a human and understandable response. The trouble with it is that it doesn't seem to be working. The women's movement surfaced the better part of a decade ago (which is almost long enough, in our era, to make it a candidate for nostalgic revival), and it is still here, still large and lively. It is also still surrounded by confusion and mixed emotions, most signally a large-scale inability to see what all the fuss is about. Complaints about the movement are many: it hasn't defined its issues clearly, it differs within itself, its goals are either Utopian or minuscule and, above all, it traffics in emotion instead of logic. Yet it persists! In fact, its reach and its backing are steadily growing.

It appears to me that we have, in this illogical situation, a very fruitful field for studying social dynamics and social mythology. If the women's movement cannot be easily contained within any set definition nor held to any stated program, perhaps that is because it is both larger and more novel than it has been thought to be. I believe that to be true. The movement seems to me to be a response to profound and irreversible historical forces involving economic, technological, and scientific shifts in our society. No wonder it hasn't yet found itself a satisfactory name or a coherent ideology! And no wonder that the psychological reactions of those who do not feel themselves involved in it are ones of bafflement and exasperation. But the disturbed emotions on one side and the unconscious drive on the other offer a rare opportunity to look at the process of human response to change while it is going on; and this I would like now to do.

Let us begin with the response, which is good clinical practice. What symptoms did the body politic display when invaded by the liberation virus? Demands for equal rights for women have produced, first, a flurry of joking and, next, some irritation and anger, but mainly and fundamentally a determination to pay no attention: a simple, almost animal, retreat into not listening. Not argument, hardly even refusal to argue, but something closer to an instinctive reflex—a refusal to *hear*.

"Playing possum" like this is a defensive mechanism which has often proved a useful tool for surviving. Women have been doing it for millennia as a defense against wanting to act when they are sure they can't, in a situation where raised consciousness are liabilities and ignorance is bliss. But if the external situation changes, blissful ignorance grows more perilous as well as more difficult. The peril is certainly not apparent as yet, but the difficulty is here. Most men still don't want to hear about the women's movement, but the buzzing goes on. A little is getting through, willy-nilly.

I think it is only natural that what is heard is largely misunderstood and what is passed on (by the men in whose hands lies the distribution of news) is mostly misrepresented because it is misunderstood. And a good deal of the time, too, the women's movement is still talking to itself. No doubt that's a necessary step in the formation of any movement: intercommunication helps to bond the group together and give it a cohesive identity, and since women are a group who have not, in recent history, had much to hold them together as a group (except outside pressure) they stand in need of a chance to learn sisterhood. Besides, talking to men who have made up their minds not to listen is a great waste of energy; and I speak as one who has addressed both listening male audiences and retreating male backs. If we look at men's reactions to the women's movement, we find it described on the one hand as absurd, and on the other as threatening. It will undermine and destroy normal relationships of all kinds, and it will also disappear tomorrow morning by ten o'clock. Its adherents are sex-mad orgiasts who (contrariwise) want to castrate men. It's a hilarious joke with no sense of humor. Women are plotting to turn the tables on men and subject them to hideous indignities; but the whole fuss is really over who washes the dishes. Anyhow, most women don't believe in the "movement" at all; it's the plaything of a handful of highly publicized exhibitionists. Black women and working-class women aren't interested, all feminists are rich, white, and bored, and my secretary likes to make me coffee just as my wife wants to stay home. And if she didn't, I'd (a) fire her and (b) divorce her.

These contradictory descriptions don't attempt serious opposition to the feminist positions. They are, rather, justifications for ignoring the whole thing. I don't set them down to argue with them, for one can't, any more than one can argue with upholders of the Flat Earth theory, if they still exist. Such descriptions are of interest because of their origin. If women are going to respond intelligently, they will need to understand the psychic sources of these disorderly reactions. Where do they come from? Why are they verbalized in these forms? What do they tell us about the distress and uneasiness which women's apparently understandable desire for equality raises in the male breast?

I believe they tell us a great deal about the effect of demands on existing power relationships to alter these relationships, and thus about the fundamental sociopolitical structure of our society. When women ask for equality, this should be seen as an example of what happens when the weak challenge the powerful. I do not believe that one can (leave "should" aside) make a Case for Women and *only* for women, and I believe that until women see this they will waste time and energy fighting all men as if every issue that arises between them were political. In my view, the case for women is a paradigm, a brief in a class action for subordinated groups as a whole against a clumsy, inefficient, and stupidly solipsistic power center. But making a case for women is particularly useful because it is novel, and thus it brings to the surface hitherto undisturbed layers of mythic mental entanglements for our investigation.

The most rational opposition to women's desire to leave their place and move into man's world lies in the pejorative definition of that world as a rat race. This is the premise to quite a good argument, a kind of Catch-23, which goes like this: If women are daft enough to want to get out of the house and into the rat race, that in itself is a very good reason for protecting them from their folly. If they can't tell when they're well off—at home, protected, guaranteed a status, a role, and an identity (while men struggle for all three in the chaotic world of action)—then obviously their tiny minds can't be trusted to handle the work of this world. Leave us men alone in our rat race where we are sacrificing ourselves to keep you women happy.

Quite a few men find this a satisfying formula and it does have a sort of specious plausibility. But *is* the world really a rat race, for the great as well as the weak? If it is, men must be credited with selfless magnanimity. If man's world offers nothing but strain and unpleasure, it seems remarkable that more men wouldn't welcome help in coping with it. When women *do* get out of their place, they are almost universally assigned to the rattiest part of the race, the drudge work. Male magnanimity seems to end at home, and the argument for keeping women there somehow comes to rest on womanly limitations per se, rather than on the unpleasantness of the world they wish to enter.

At once we are back in a contradictory muddle, for the limitations of woman's nature, as usually presented, oppose each other. Women are defined on the one hand as too gentle and fine to do man's work, and on the other as too indecisive, slow, and self-centered. If the two objections are lumped together to say simply that women aren't fitted for man's world, we are still faced with a contradiction from another familiar argument, that their competition will be tough enough to take jobs away from deserving men. This tangle of contradictions suggests that rationalization has usurped the place of reason. When men say, "You don't belong here," they mean, "We don't want you here." I am not surprised that women get angry at that (though it is the first time in history that they *have* got angry at it, which is one reason men are surprised and discountenanced), and their anger will help to reinforce their desire for change. But no one can work effectively for change simply by looking at her own side of the question. If the opposition to equality for women is contradictory, that means its roots run deep, and straightforward argument won't change anything, by itself. If men would be better off listening to women, women would be better off seeing their cause in context.

And, of course, the concept of woman as mystery, woman as "other," is not the only justification in men's minds for their opposition to equality between the sexes. Certainly it's a primary obstacle, as Simone de Beauvoir saw and said long ago. But there's another catch which is less familiar and perhaps less obvious because it is contained within the very term "equality." What does reaching equality mean? For a woman, it is a *step up,* to a level where, like men, she will be in better control of her life and find her ambitions limited by fewer *a priori* barriers.

Unfortunately, and women don't often see this, a step up for women will be seen by many men as a step *down* for men to an inferior level, woman's level. To these men, and they are a vast majority, equality doesn't mean, "A woman is as good as I am"; it means, "I'm no better than she is." Equality *for* women brings more competition, but for those who think of themselves as fair competitors, that isn't shattering. Equality *with* women, however, is something else. If you have been brought up to know that women are inferior—deservedly inferior—how can you accept that? It's shocking, it's insulting, it's UNFAIR.

Worse still—and here we come back to the hidden terror haunting men—doesn't an acceptance of the equality of women cut men off (most men, nondominant men) from the alliance with the powerful which that handy old slogan, "It's a

Elizabeth Janeway

man's world," seems to validate? To divide the world by sex is to bind males—both weak and powerful—together by means of the destiny of anatomy. Take that alliance away, and equate the men who stand outside the elite with women, and you are telling them that they can expect to be treated *like* women, objects, and "others," not doers but done to; and done to, yes, right down to sexual doing. Closing the male/female split means a drastic rearrangement of the barriers between the weak and the powerful. Then not women, but the weak, become the second sex, subordinate, submissive, subject to rape.

Alliance with women removes from men the protection of maleness against rape by the powerful; and though, in our society, the fear of rape by men of men is not often acknowledged, it exists. James Dickey's novel *Deliverance* tapped that fear and gained great force by so doing. The premise underlying this fear is quite clear: if power has no bounds, it will extend to physical misuse. The paradigmatic act of the powerful, performed upon the weak, is rape.

Now, rape need not always be performed by force. In fact, one of the charms of pornography is that it records session after session of guiltless rape in which the powerful are licensed to have their will of the weak because the weak "really like it that way." *Last Tango in Paris* offers a contemporary example which makes brilliant use of currently resonant themes. It is a story of encounter between strangers, which is a fundamental and haunting situation for us today. It is also a situation that invites mythic interpretation because the individual personalities of the man and woman involved are erased, leaving only the central nub of their sexual presence. Only symbolic rape is present here, because the woman accepts subordination and asks for abuse; but we can regard it as psychologically equivalent to physical rape because the relationship involves dominance of female by male to the point which our society usually considers degrading. This is not a matter of moral judgment, but of aesthetics. There is no doubt that the audience is intended to be shocked, and is shocked, by the man's demands and the woman's acquiescence. The heroine—and she is not presented as an individual but rather as a mythic projection of "what they really like"— is depicted as wanting degradation and returning willingly to the male in order to receive it. Even in everyday life, her fiancé is making her the heroine of a documentary film, that is, he's forcing an individual identity on her, and she doesn't like it.

The element of myth is further underlined by the fact that the man has nothing to sustain his superiority except his maleness, which is depicted as his ability to dominate to degradation the girl he meets by chance, and the depersonalized universality of the situation is increased by his insistence on anonymity between them. We are down on bedrock, says this demanding and brilliant film, on physical confrontation outside social norms, a confrontation that can stand for any encounter between man and woman. The lesson of the film is that male superiority is based on dominance of the female, an idyll acted out in a vacuum in obedience to magical law. She is young, beautiful, better-class, indeed, privileged; and none of that matters. In the idyll, in the myth, her pleasure is his power, and his power is shown by her degradation. She wants it that way, just as she does not want the exaltation of her individuality that her film-making boyfriend is forcing on her. Incidentally, he is sufficiently male—dominant over her himself—to be doing this without her permission. Either way she is being manipulated.

In the end, as actuality begins to break in with his threat of telling his name and following her home, the truth of the myth is menaced. Life-as-it-is—or rather life-as-it-is according to the film—rises up against life-as-it-ought-to-be. In life-as-it-is, the woman must release herself from the submission she really desires; but she is not strong enough to do so merely by sending her lover away. He is dominant. He won't go. She can free herself only by violence. Even her privileged and protected position cannot make her his equal, and she can win back her autonomy and reassert her identity only by breaking the law which is not strong enough to protect her from him, by killing him—leaving us with the moral that it is a law of nature that men are dominant over women, and the only means by which women can, even temporarily and willfully, reverse this edict is by murder. Or, to say it the other way around, equality is nonsense, and women who ask for it are liars who will end by slaughtering men.

If we try to sort out this visceral response to the women's movement, I think we can discern three stages of opposition. The first results from the fact that the movement raises the question of power. It is not simply, or even fundamentally, the demand that women be given a share in power that upsets men; it is that this demand forces upon men a review of their own position. If women are announcing themselves ready to storm the bastions of the Establishment, where does that leave the men who have failed to do so? who have settled down to live out their lives in submission and resignation? And that includes, one way or another, the great majority of men. Suddenly, past the doors of their cells, bursting out of the slave quarters, come women-the-inferiors, invading the corridors of power as if, by merely being human, they had a right to be there. But most men have given up that right in return for a quiet life and some sense of security, for government by law as an acceptable bargain between the weak and the powerful. The idea that women are now refusing to accept this bargain acts as a terrifying, a paralyzing, challenge to men. Either they too must revolt or they must acknowledge themselves lacking in the courage and ambition being shown by their traditionally inferior sisters.

Role-changing, I wrote in *Man's World, Woman's Place,* is hard on everyone but hardest on those members of a relationship who have not themselves initiated the changes in the role relations which they share. It's true that role-changers have troubles. Today women who are attempting new roles still find it a daunting challenge to value themselves and their experience and ambitions as seriously as they do those of men. Doubting themselves, they can make unnerving mistakes, fall into negation and the mere reversal of old attitudes instead of working out creative new approaches to the demands of changed reality, and sometimes they despair. But men are worse handicapped by the fact that, in today's shifts in sex roles, they are not the initiators. Women are motivated and often very strongly so. To the extent that they can contain and control the drive and anger they feel, it helps them. Men, however, would rather have had things left as they were; which means that in the present situation they are actually experiencing the unpleasant sensation of being done to instead of doing, and the anger they perceive among women is frightening. They don't understand that it comes out of past frustration and assume, naturally enough, that it is an augury of future dominance. This observation seems still true, but when I wrote it I had not seen the further point I am making now: the changes women demand are compelling men to rethink their relationship not just to women but to the whole power structure of our society. It is a hard and unwelcome task.

Secondly, there is the very real problem that women's demands mean different things to men from what they mean to women. We have seen how that works with the apparently fair demand for equality. The same difficulty dogs another seemingly uncomplicated statement made by women, of their similarity as human beings. We are not "others," say women, we are human beings like you in whom there exists merely a happenstantial sex difference. We acknowledge that difference, but why should it apply to more than sex? Why should it signify across-the-board differences of nature and capability? Anatomy is not destiny; it is simply anatomy. Let us be whole human beings together, accepting differences between us as individual excellences or defects, not determinants of character.

But the ability of women to see themselves as human beings first and females only second is the product of a change in women's life-experience which has not yet, at any rate, been matched by a corresponding change in men's lives. The acceptance by women of a self-image totally different from the male's is diminishing as women's life-styles become more like those of men. In the last few months I have gone over a mass of newspaper clippings culled from *The New York Times* in the years from the 1890s to the present, relating to women and their activities. The long-term trend reveals a marked shift in the image of women that emerges: women are more and more seen as approaching the capable, active, involved human norm and leaving "otherness" behind. Their interests grow wider. They are assumed to arrive at their own decisions more frequently. They stop being adjuncts of parents or husbands. The jobs open to them shift from the most menial (salesgirls, domestics working for pittances, seamstresses, factory operatives, addressers of envelopes) toward the white-collar area, and then beyond it. Eighty years ago, marriage was not just the goal presented as proper to every young girl; marriage without parental consent might well involve elopement: which means that a marriageable girl was still something of an object of barter between father and husband. Fifty years ago, a daring middle-class girl could become a secretary without being immediately declassed. The advantage she gained, however, was not independence, but rather freedom from the absolute necessity of accepting the first man who asked her hand in marriage. Her job was not thought of as a career, but as a chance to build up a dowry for herself and gain her a better choice of marriage partner. Career women were things apart, and not expected to marry at all.

Today, middle-class women are very much somewhere else. I have talked to enough of them in the last three years, in cities and small towns across the country, to bear witness to the transformation. If middle-class ideals are still influential, we must factor into American attitudes the idea that growing up and getting married to Mr. Right is now a very old-fashioned dream. It's a nice idea, but it isn't enough. The normal expectation now includes some kind of career-vocation-job which will continue to occupy and interest one throughout life, which is simply to say that women now, more than ever before, see their lives as being much more like the lives of men.

This shift of image is more than mere wishful thinking. The women's movement is a response to fundamental social and economic changes, changes that are long-term, continuing, and which affect women's lives both inside and outside the home. The number and proportion of women in the labor force grow every year. The proportion now stands at 40 percent and gives the push toward upper-level jobs a basis in logic and practice that didn't exist at the time of the first feminist wave. Young women are moving into the professions at a faster and faster clip. The increasing numbers of women law students who began their studies in 1970 are hitting the job market now and will become more obvious every year. Applications to medical school among women have also begun to rise. Young women in industry are less and less willing to be shunted off into lower-management jobs, with top-level promotion going to a token few. In politics, women are increasingly active at neighborhood, county, and municipal levels, where they are able to command a power base that is not dependent on tactical appointment by male bosses. In time, they will move up.

This is the experience behind the questioning of happy-wife-and-motherdom as a total goal. Underlining the experience is the reason for it. Most of these women workers are not out in man's world primarily to find self-fulfillment. They are working because their families need the money. Very few men really grasp the fact that working women rarely have an option to work or not. Too many discussions of women at work assume they could all stay home if they wanted to. But six million women are heads of households, and at least sixteen million more bring in the wages that keep their families above the poverty line. With prices of food and fuel and housing and transport and education climbing steadily, more and more families are coming to depend on a second paycheck. Publicly rather than privately, the income of working wives has been a very important source of economic growth in America since the war, perhaps the most important. If a growth economy makes jobs, which is a fundamental tenet of our American creed, these working women are making jobs for men and other women, not cutting men out of the labor force.

It's true that most women at work are working in women's jobs, which are definable as routine, dead-end, and low-paid. But they are jobs in man's world, and that means that women's lives are coming more and more to approximate men's lives, particularly, of course, the lives of nondominant men who are also likely to hold the more routine and lower-paid jobs. The effect of this pattern on women is to reduce their sense of themselves as deserving that label of "other." In the workaday world, what distinguishes them from men is not their sex so much as their failure to hold and exercise power, a distinction that seems to bring them closer to the men who fall at the lower end of the power spectrum.

To many men, however, this identification of interests does not exist. Some of the toughest opposition to the equal rights amendment has been mounted by unions, an interesting measure of the depth of repugnance within nondominant men toward the idea of equality with women. Union leaders who *prefer* a divided labor movement to giving women equality (and a shot at overtime pay) are clearly motivated by forces beyond the reach of logic.

The third aspect of the opposition by nondominant men to women's demands is grounded in men's need to retain the image of woman as "other." That's connected, of course, with the idea of woman as inferior, most obviously (as De Beauvoir pointed out) because if you are the *first* sex, you will be the setter of norms, not the deviates who must be defined in "other" terms. But being "other" signifies a great many things besides being inferior, and these aspects of "otherness" quite often seem to men to have positive values. Women who want to be regarded as human beings first, and female only incidentally, upset the old, long-standing value system in what seems to men an ungracious and ungrateful way. This lapse is what provokes all those jokes about opening doors and pulling out chairs and rising when a woman enters the room, for these gestures have been the honorifics, so to speak, of the traditional male/female relationship, pointing up the sex difference. The to-do about minor manners seems nonsensical to rational women, but when we maintain that, we are being simpleminded, not rational. Minor manners could give rise to such a fuss only by symbolizing something else, something important.

Indeed, Professor Laurel Richardson Walum of Ohio State University enlivened the proceedings of last fall's meeting of the American Sociological Association by delivering a paper on "The Changing Door Ceremony." Professor Walum's students were enlisted to invade public places and deliberately violate the regular ritual of door-opening, in which the female modestly steps aside, "demonstrating frailty, ineptitude, and a need for protection," and waits till the male opens the door, thus displaying "the male virtues of physical strength, mechanical ability, worldliness, self-confidence, and efficacy." Who would have thought so much could be read from door ritual? But its violation produced confusion and embarrassment, and allowed Professor Walum to conclude that "the hand that holds the door-knob rules the world."

But why do men need to have women accept the role of "other"? What positive value can there be to such a position? I believe that the value lies not just in pushing women out of competition in man's world, but in the fact that this apartness serves to keep alive a different system of values, another set of norms and goods. "Others" (women) serve as repositories for ideals and life-styles which men feel they cannot themselves take on, but which, they suspect, may have some potential usefulness. These values have been significant in the past and sometimes are still given lip service as virtues. And while they haven't much relevance to one's day-to-day activity, one doesn't quite like to kill them off.

Let us glance at one. In an earlier age, most normal human beings (that is, men) were unable to disguise from themselves the fact of their inequality with the power-elite, an unpleasant fact which is rather better hidden today by our relative affluence and our less oppressive political system. When such inequality was a constant aspect of daily life, Christian humility was a socially useful ideal, often preached and sometimes practiced. For the oppressed, it justified their oppression, and thus allowed those who might otherwise have foundered in shame to support lives they could not change.

If it is argued that they could have changed their lives by successful, determined revolt, and that Christian humility functioned to keep them from revolting, I can counter only by saying that, in fact, it didn't. Other, millennial Christian ideals nurtured a long series of peasant rebellions, all of which were ultimately unsuccessful. As long as rebellions were doomed to failure, the ideal of humility had the positive value of shielding those who had failed from seeing themselves as failures. At the point when modern times and technology made it possible for rebellions to succeed—sometime in the eighteenth century— humility became a virtue not so much of the weak per se as of women. And since it may become useful once again, at some future date, it remains a part of the female hoard of virtues, stored for safekeeping till needed.

One function of "otherness," then, is social, to preserve archaic attitudes and once-useful character traits against a day when they may once more meet a need. Concomitantly, the personal use to men of woman-as-other (and honor again to De Beauvoir for her exposition of the point) is as a locus for projection by the First Sex of its desires, needs, and fears, so that emotions which can't be allowed full play in "real life" can be somehow absorbed or transformed. All wives and most secretaries expect to be dumped on now and then, not just as confidantes to whom frustrations can be reported but as surrogates on whom they can be vented. Not that all the emotions projected onto women by men are angry, any more than they are all lustful urges toward sex objects. Woman-as-other provides a focus for many needs and yearnings: for tenderness, given and asked for, for maternal protection, for divine assurance, for support against forces of depersonalization, for evidence of the existence of self-sacrifice and loving-kindness. Women are thought of by men as (and thus they are instructed to be) upholders and transmitters of high virtues and values. They are validators of emotions and interpreters of experience. To men, this seems a role of great dignity and nobility, an elevation. Why do women refuse the pedestal?

How very hard it is for women to make clear that by becoming a terribly necessary aspect of someone else's life, one ceases to be a person in oneself. To accept that one is "other" rather than human is to deny one's identity *as* a human and feel one's own personality as obtrusive, clouding the mirror one is supposed to be.

And how very hard it is for men to accept women's need to take on the unworthy (it seems to them) everydayness of mere human personality! For if women are simply people, no better and no worse than men, where are men's dreams to roost? Who will forgive them for their trespasses? Who will accept the sins they cannot accept themselves, minister to the needs that shame them, reflect their view of the world back to them unchanged and so make it real, echo their curses and confirm their creeds? Isn't that power? men ask. What more do they want?

To come back for a moment to *Last Tango in Paris*, we should regard it not just as a counter-assertion against women's demands, but as an expression of need. It declares that the acquiescence of women in men's sexual acts—that is, in their desperate reach for transcendence and a connection to the sacred—is the way men validate their sense of themselves, of their very right to exist and enforce demands and be assuaged for pain and anger and frustration, and that this right is paramount, essential to life. The existence of power depends on the right to dominate. Take it away, and men will cease to be men, which means that by "becoming men" women are threatening men with "becoming women"—that is, with having to acknowledge no identity except that shared one of weakness.

The powerful male, of course, dominates easily and is shielded from constant frustration. The weak men, who suffer daily hurt, know what it is to be inferior. For them, women have become the only territory on which their daring and drive can prove itself. And so, for them, woman must be "other," a nameless and faceless creature with the right to say Yes, but not No. We see these fantasies spelled out in *Playboy* and *Penthouse* and the other magazines of this nature. They normalize the premises of pornography and assure their readers that dominance is right, by surrounding these battered egos with a world full of female puppets who can be clothed in dreams and desires without intruding unwelcome personalities. The women's movement can see all that, but what it overlooks is the need behind it, the terrible need to dominate *something.* If your sense of inferiority persuades you that you can't successfully dominate another human being, you are going to try to find a puppet.

In Baton Rouge, Louisiana, where I visited this past flood season, the equal rights amendment was coming up for discussion in the legislature. Its support is largely respectable and middle-class—rational, I guess you'd say. Its opposition runs a gamut, but it certainly reaches beyond the rational. The night before I arrived in town, a furious female opponent had taken to the airwaves and castigated the local chapter of the National Organization of Women (which in Baton Rouge is about as radical as the League of Women Voters) for upholding homosexuality and aiming to castrate normal males. The members of NOW whom I met were almost more astounded by the attack than they were angry, and one saw—as with Nixon's henchmen when Watergate brought them to the surface—how useful the numbing shock effect of calculated effrontery can be. But Madame X was not simply outrageous; she was aiming her outrages well, for she invoked the deep fear that equality for women means that men will be treated *like* women, will be faced with the alternatives of choosing to act the woman's sexual role (homosexuality) or being turned into eunuchs by castration. To admit one's equality with women means taking on membership in the second sex among creatures who are not quite human, who are not protected by bonds of fellow feeling, whose alliance with the powerful has been lost and, with it, their protection against use and misuse, and abuse of all sorts. It means sporting a badge as engulfing of hope and possibilities as the yellow star Jews wore in Hitler's Germany.

Put at its simplest, men whose experience has taught them that equality between weak and powerful doesn't exist find it intensely difficult to imagine that admitting women to equality will not somehow jeopardize their own insecure position. The idea that joining with women to oppose the power structure might be profitable is regarded as ludicrous: how could you profit by taking on an ally weaker than yourself? Your losses, on the contrary, are clear: the only sure security you have is that guaranteed by women's inferior place. Dissolving the sex difference will accentuate the power difference. It will drop you into the limbo where exploitation doesn't just happen, it is sanctioned.

To say these are nightmare fears doesn't make them easier to deal with. Can they be dealt with at all? Or is the nascent women's movement going to spawn a bitter and disruptive backlash that will stop it in its tracks? There is, of course, no easy answer. We are certainly going to get some backlash, though more important than verbal attack will be the continuance of inaction which the attacks serve to justify. The idea that women are going to climb easily into positions of power because fairness demands that they be represented according to their numbers is naïve; and, in fact, few women take seriously government rulings on equal employment as effective in themselves. They will have to be invoked and enforced by repeated court action. But despair over the prospect is also naïve, because so much has already happened. The economic and technological base for a world polarized by sex into dual systems of occupation and behavior began to vanish years ago. The strength of the women's movement doesn't lie in its rhetoric, but in the fact that it is a response (diverse and unorganized still, and the better for it) to changed realities. One such reality is a very different kind of family structure from what we still frame as ideal, much reduced in sheer numbers, reduced in necessary or useful activities, in specialness—the tide of television gives children a common, non-family-related world of experience as soon as they can talk—and greatly reduced in active relations to a wider community. Such relations are now individual, not made as a family group.

Economic needs now pull families apart instead of supporting their existence as working groups. Working mothers and wives aren't new, but today they must leave the home to earn; and though that too began years ago, only in the last generation has support to working mothers from relatives, neighbors, and hired help dwindled to practically zero. The demand for child-care centers, for example, is forced on women by the present situation. For most working mothers the alternative is untrained baby sitters, custodial day care with other untrained women in their homes—or the street and an empty (except for TV) apartment.

Equally, the isolation of the family has reinforced the effort to bring fathers closer into child care and housework. It's a response (good in itself but inadequate) to the lack of community support for the family and to our American social mobility that separates young couples from their families. Communes and cluster-living may help in time, but they are not only still disapproved socially, they seem to many to involve too great a loss of privacy. To be brief, a great many of our widespread contemporary problems have surfaced first, or in slightly different but acute form, in women's lives because they affect the family drastically. All too often they have been seen exclusively as family problems, personal dilemmas. The isolation of women from one another, each tucked away in her nuclear family, leaves a woman to grope with difficulties that may well have been thrust on her by society in the belief that she can solve them by herself. One real reward that the women's movement has brought us all is the increasing realization that a lot of family upsets are not unique, but instead the result of social dislocations. Understanding the nature of these upsets makes them easier to cope with because it not only brings in the social context, it gets rid of personal guilt.

Women can't solve these problems by themselves, or by male/female argument. They are bound up with the accepted social system as sustained by the power structure. But women at least are aware of them. I believe that intelligent men will start listening harder to what women are telling them about the realities they find themselves facing, once they understand that these are offshoots of larger difficulties that show themselves in other areas.

For what it's worth, my own feeling about the future of the sexes is hopeful. Partly my optimism is based on as objective and historical-minded a judgment as I can come to. The fact that men's and women's lives are becoming more alike seems to me to open doors to understanding and affectionate friendship between them. In addition, the increased ability of women to look after themselves as independent beings suggests that when they give love, it will be real love, not a hypocritical sham exacted by their dependence and often hiding secret resentment. I don't at all believe, as Erich Fromm does, that polarization of the sexes is necessary for a sound relationship between them. At any rate, it doesn't guarantee it, or how explain the large amount of homosexuality present in two such polarized societies as Periclean Greece and Victorian England? No, it seems to me that getting rid of sexual stereotypes can only enlarge the variety of *petites différences* which add a spice to affection.

Beyond objectivity, I find myself unable to ignore my old novelist's sense of mood. I have met an awful lot of liberated women in the last three years, and the constant impression they make is sheer enjoyment of life and good-feeling with each other. That is indeed a personal reaction, but it may be worth recording as an offset to the constant recurrence of sad tales about unhappy and lonesome women who have chosen feminism and therefore (!) left their mates, to their everlasting regret. The New York press seems rather to specialize in these cautionary fables; and while I don't agree with Spiro Agnew's view of effete Eastern journalism, it is only fair to say that things seemed different in Arkansas, Wisconsin, Louisiana, Oregon, and Iowa; in Missouri, Florida, Virginia, Michigan, Massachusetts, western Pennsylvania, upstate New York, and some way stations that I have overlooked. Most of the women I have run into and talked with are married, or see no reason why they may not be; lots of them have children; they are coping with jobs or with studies too, and they have been overwhelmingly energetic, cheerful, funny, and good-natured. They were also, those I met, of all ages, many backgrounds, and several colors. Discount my impression by all means, by whatever amount you desire, but it was everywhere the same, and everywhere positive.

Out of this experience and cogitation let me make two recommendations for future discourse between the sexes. I think women would do well to widen the context in which they see their needs and present their demands. A change in sex roles is a challenge to personal dominance and to political power both; to men as individuals and to a male caste which has a stake in separating itself from women, or at least thinks it has. I believe also that women would profit by a study of power and its workings. They might even produce some effective new techniques just because they come fresh to macro-politics, but they also need to see how such political action differs from private tussles over domination in the personal sphere.

As for men, I suggest that more of them listen more to women, and listen with the possibility in mind that some of what women say may not only be serious but even sensible. For the first time in history, perhaps, it is women's experience which is changing faster and more radically than that of men. In itself that bears witness to the profundity of the changes, and it might alert men to the value of taking a look at them. Certainly it will not be easy to overcome men's fears of the effects of change in woman's role and image, but these fears are grounded in a mythology that is less and less in tune with social actuality. Mythologies do change as their support falls away, and perhaps we might find some cheer in the fact that men who habitually work with women, as equals in man's world, seem to be less disturbed by the ideas of equality for women than men who don't. In part, men's fear of equality is based on ignorance of how such a situation would work in practice. Our best evidence that the situation can work comes from the experience of those who have been living with it, and that seems to me realistically heartening.

Doris Lessing
NOT A VERY NICE STORY

This story is difficult to tell. Where to put the emphasis? Whose perspective to use? For to tell it from the point of view of the lovers (but that was certainly not their word for themselves—from the viewpoint then of the guilty couple), it is as if a lie were to be described through the eyes of some person who scarcely appeared in it; as if a cousin from Canada had visited, let's say, a farmer in Cornwall half a dozen unimportant times, and then wrote as if these meetings had been the history of the farm and the family. Or it is as if a stretch of years were to be understood in terms of the extra day in Leap Year.

To put it conventionally is simple: two marriages, both as happy as marriages are, both exemplary from society's point of view, contained a shocking flaw, a secret cancer, a hidden vice.

But this hidden horror did not rot the marriages, and seemed hardly to matter at all: the story can't be told as the two betrayed ones saw it; they didn't see it. They saw nothing. There would be nothing to tell.

Now, all this was true for something like twenty years; then something happened which changed the situation. To be precise, what happened was the death of one of the four people concerned. But at any moment during those twenty years, what has been said would have been true; conventional morality would judge these marriages to have a secret face, all lies and lust; from the adulterers' point of view, what they did was not much more important than sharing a taste for eating chocolate after the doctor has said no.

After that death, however, the shift of emphasis: the long unimportance of the twenty years of chocolate-eating could be seen as a prelude to something very different; could be seen as heartless frivolity or callousness redeemed providentially by responsibility. But suppose the death had not occurred?

It is hard to avoid the thought that all these various ways of looking at the thing are nonsense. . . .

Frederick Jones married Althea; Henry Smith married Muriel, at the same time, that is, in 1947. Both men, both women, had been much involved in the war, sometimes dangerously. But now it was over, they knew that it had been the way it had gone on and on that had affected them most. It had been endless.

There is no need to say much about their emotions when they married. Frederick and Althea, Henry and Muriel, felt exactly as they might be expected to feel, being their sort of people—middle-class, liberal, rather literary—and in their circumstances, which emotionally consisted of hungers of all kinds, but particularly for security, affection, warmth, these hungers having been heightened beyond normal during the long war. They were all four aware of their condition, were able to see themselves with the wryly tolerant eye of their kind. For they at all times knew to a fraction of a degree the state of their emotional pulse, and were much given to intelligent discussions about their individual psychologies.

Yet in spite of views about themselves which their own parents would have regarded as intolerable to live with, their plans and aims for themselves were similar to those of their parents at the same age. Both couples wished and expected that their marriages would be the bedrock of their lives, that they would have children and bring them up well. And it turned out as they wanted. They also expected that they would be faithful to each other.

At the time these marriages took place, the couples had not met. Both Doctor Smith and Doctor Jones, separately, had had the idea of going into partnership and possibly founding a clinic in a poor area. Both had been made idealists by the war, even socialists of a nonidealogical sort. They advertised, made contact by letter, liked each other, and bought a practice in a country town in the west of England where there would be many poor people to look after, as well as the rich.

Houses were bought, not far from each other. While the two men were already friends, with confidence in their being able to work together, the wives had not met. It was agreed that it was high time this event should take place. An occasion was to be made of it. The four were to meet for dinner in a pub five miles outside the little town. That they should all get on well was known by them to be important. In fact, both women had made small humorous complaints that if their "getting on" was really considered so important, then why had their meeting been left so late?—this was the real reason for the special dinner.

As the two cars drove up to the country inn, the same state of affairs prevailed in each. There was bad humor. The women felt they were being patronized, the men felt that the women were probably right but were being unreasonable in making a fuss when after all the main thing was to get settled in work and in their homes. All four were looking forward to that dinner—the inn was known for its food—while for their different reasons they resented being there at all. They arrived in each other's presence vivid with variegated emotions. The women at once knew they liked each other—but after all, they might very well have not liked each other!—and made common cause about the men. The four went into the bar, where they were an animated and combative group.

By the time they moved into the dining room, ill humor had vanished. There they sat, with their wine and good food. They were attracting attention, because they were obviously dressed up for a special occasion, but chiefly because of their own consciousness of well-being. This was the peak of their lives; the long tedium of the war was over; the men were still in their early thirties, the women in their twenties. They were feeling as if at last their real lives were starting. They were all good-looking. The men were of the same type: jokes had been made about that already. They were both dark, largely built, with the authority of doctors, "comfortable" as the wives said. And the women were pretty. They soon established (like showing each other their passports or references of decency and reliability) that they shared views on life—tough, but rewarding; God—dead; children—to be brought up with the right blend of permissiveness and discipline; society—to be cured by common sense and mild firmness but without extremes of any sort.

Everything was well for them; everything would get better.

They sat a long time over their food, their wine, and their happiness, and left only when the pub closed, passing into a cold, clear night, frost on the ground. It happened that conversations between Frederick Jones and Muriel Smith, Althea Jones and Henry Smith, were in progress, and the couples, so arranged, stood by their respective cars.

"Come back to us for a nightcap," said Henry, assisting his colleague's wife in beside him, and drove off home.

Frederick and Muriel, not one word having been said, watched them go, then turned to each other and embraced. This embrace can best be described as being the inevitable continuation of their conversation. Frederick then drove a few hundred yards into a small wood, where the frost shone on the grass; stopped the car, flung down his coat, and then he and Muriel made love—no, that's not right—had sex, with vigor and relish and enjoyment, while nothing lay between them and their nakedness and some degrees of frost but a layer of tweed. They then dressed, got back into the car, and went back to town, where Frederick drove Muriel to her own home, came in with her for the promised nightcap, and took his own wife home.

Both married couples made extensive love that night, as the atmosphere all evening had promised they would.

Muriel and Frederick did not examine their behavior as much as such compulsive examiners of behavior might have been expected to do. The point was, the incident was out of character, unlike them, so very much *not* what they believed in, that they didn't know what to think about it, let alone what to feel. Muriel had always set her face against the one-night stand. Trivial, she had said it was—the word *sordid* was overemphatic. Frederick, both professionally and personally, had a lot to say about the unsatisfactory nature of casual sexual relationships. In his consulting room he would show carefully measured disapproval for the results—venereal disease or pregnancy—of such relations. It was not a moral judgment he was making, he always said; no, it was a hygienic one. He had been heard to use the word "messy." Both these people had gone in, one could say on principle, for the serious affair, the deep involvement. Even in wartime, neither had had casual sex.

So while it was hardly possible that such extraordinary behavior could be forgotten, neither thought about it: the incident could not be included in their view of themselves.

And besides, there was so much to do, starting the new practice, arranging the new homes.

Besides, too, both couples were so pleased with each other, and had such a lot of love to make.

About six weeks after that evening at the pub, Frederick had to drop in to Henry and Muriel's to pick up something, and found Muriel alone. Again, not one word having been said, they went to the bedroom and—but I think the appropriate word here is *screwed*. Thoroughly and at length.

They parted; and again unable to understand themselves, let the opportunity to think about what had happened slide away.

The thing was too absurd! They could not say, for instance, that during that famous evening at the pub, when they first met, that they had eyed each other with incipient desire, or had sent out messages of need or intent. They had not done more than to say to themselves, as one does: I'd like to make love with that man/woman if I wasn't well-suited already. They certainly could not have said that during the intervening six weeks they had dreamed of each other, finding their actual partners unsatisfactory. Far from it.

For if these, Muriel and Frederick, were natural sexual partners, then so were Frederick and Althea, Henry and Muriel.

If we now move on ten years and look back, as the guilty couple, Frederick and Muriel then did—or rather, as both couples did, ten years being a natural time or place for such compulsive self-examiners to make profit-and-loss accounts—it is only in an effort to give the right emphasis to the thing.

Doris Lessing

For it is really hard to get the perspective right. Suppose that I had, in fact, described the emotions of the two very emotional courtships, the emotional and satisfying affairs that preceeded marriage, the exciting discoveries of marriage and the depths and harmonies both couples found, and had then said, simply: On many occasions two of these four people commited adultery, without forethought or afterthought, and these adulterous episodes, though extremely enjoyable, had no effect whatever on the marriages—thus making them sound something like small bits of grit in mouthfuls of honey. Well, but even the best of marriages can hardly be described as honey. Perhaps it is that word *adultery*—too weighty? Redolent of divorces and French farce? Yet it is still in use, very much so: it is a word that people think, and not only in the law courts.

Perhaps, to get the right emphasis, insofar as those sexual episodes were having an effect on the marriages, one might as well not mention them at all. But not to mention them is just as impossible—apart from what happened in the end, the end of the story. For surely it is absolutely outside what we all know to be psychologically possible for the partners of happy marriages, both of them founded on truth and love and total commitment, to have casual sex with close mutual friends— thus betraying their marriages, their relationships, themselves—and for these betrayals to have no effect on them at all.

No guilt? No private disquiet? What was felt when gazing into their loving partners' eyes, with everything open and frank between them? Frederick, Muriel, had to think: How can I treat my trusting partner like this?

They had no such thoughts. For ten years the marriages had prospered side by side. The Joneses had produced three children, the Smiths two. The young doctors worked hard, as doctors do. In the two comfortable gardened houses, the two attractive young wives worked as hard as wives and mothers do. And all that time the marriages were being assessed by very different standards, which had nothing to do with those trivial and inelegant acts of sex—which continued whenever circumstances allowed, quite often, though neither guilty partner searched for occasions—all that time the four people continued to take their emotional pulses, as was their training: the marriages were satisfactory; no, not so satisfactory; yes, very good again. It was better in the second year than in the first, but less good in the third than in the fourth. The children brought the couples closer together in some ways, but not in others—and so on. Frederick was glad he had married delightful and sexy little Althea; and she was glad she had married Frederick, whose calm strength was her admirable complement. And Henry was pleased with Muriel, so vivacious, fearless, and self-sufficing; and Muriel was similarly glad she had chosen Henry, whose quietly humorous mode of dealing with life always absorbed any temporary disquiets she might be suffering.

All four, of course, would sometimes wonder if they should have married at all, in the way everyone does; and all four would discuss with themselves and with each other, or as a foursome, the ghastliness of marriage as an institution and how it should be abolished and something else put in its place. Sometimes, in the grip of a passing attraction for someone else, all four might regret their choices were now narrowed down to one. (At such times neither Frederick nor Muriel thought of each other; they took each other for granted, since they were always available to each other, like marriage partners.) In short, and to be done with it, at the end of ten years, and during the soul-searching and bookkeeping that went on then, both couples could look back on marriages that had in every way fulfilled what they had expected, even in the way of "taking the rough with the smooth." For where is the pleasure in sweet-without-sour? In spite of, because of, sexually exciting times and chilly times, of temporary hostilities and harmonies, of absences and illnesses, of yearning, briefly, for others—because of all this they had enjoyed a decade of profoundly emotional experience. In joy or in pain, they could not complain about flatness, or absence of sensation. And after all, emotion is the thing, we can none of us get enough of it.

What transports the couples had suffered! What tears the two women had wept! What long delicious nights spent on

---

prolonged sexual pleasure! What quarrels and crises and dramas! What depth of experience everywhere! And now the five children, each one an emotion in itself, each one an extension of emotion, claiming the future for similar pleasurable or at least sensational rivers of feeling.

It was round about the eleventh year that there came a moment of danger to them all. Althea fell in love with a young doctor who had come to help in the practice while the two senior doctors took leave. The two families usually took holidays together, but this time the men went off tramping in Scotland, leaving the women and children.

Althea confided in Muriel. It was not a question of leaving her Frederick: certainly not. She could bear to hurt neither him nor the children. But she was suffering horribly, from desire and all kinds of suddenly discovered deprivations, for the sake of the young man with whom she had slept half a dozen times furtively—horrible word!—when the children were playing in the garden or were asleep at night. Her whole life seemed a desert of dust and ashes. She could not bear the future. What was the point of living?

The two young women sat talking in Althea's kitchen.

They were at either end of the breakfast table around which so many jolly occasions had been shared by them all. Althea was weeping.

Perhaps this is the place to describe these two women. Althea was a small, round, dark creature, who always smelled delightful, and who was described by her husband as the most eminently satisfactory blend of femininity and common sense. As for Muriel, she was a strong, large-boned woman, fair, with the kind of skin that tans quickly, so that she always looked very healthy. Her clothes were of the kind called casual, and she took a lot of trouble over them. Both women, of course, often yearned to be like the other.

These two different women sat stirring coffee cups as they had done a hundred times, while the five children shouted, competed, and loved in the garden, and Althea wept, because she said this was a watershed in her marriage, like eating the apple in Eden. If she told her beloved husband that she was— temporarily, she did so hope and believe—besottedly in love with this young doctor, then it must be the end of everything between them. But if she didn't tell him, then it was betrayal. Whatever she did would have terrible results. *Not* telling Frederick seemed to her worse even than the infidelity itself. She had never, ever concealed anything from him. Perfect frankness and sincerity had been their rule—no, not a rule, they had never had to lay down rules for behavior that came so excellently and simply out of their love and trust. She could not imagine keeping anything from Frederick. And she was sure he told her everything. She could not bear it, would certainly leave him at once, if she knew that he had ever lied to her. No, she would not mind infidelity of a certain kind— how could she mind?—now that she forfeited any rights in the matter! But lies, deceptions, furtiveness—no, that would be the end, the end of everything.

Althea and Muriel stayed together, while one woman wept and talked and the other listened, stopping only when the children came in, for all that day, and all the next, and for several after that. For Muriel was understanding that it was the words and tears that were the point, not what was said: soon the energy of suffering, the tension of conflict, would have spent itself, making it all seem less important. But Muriel was determined not to listen for one minute more than was necessary. And soon she was able to advise Althea, the tears having abated, not to tell her Fred anything at all; she would just have to learn to live with a lie.

And now of course she had to think, really to think, whether she liked it or not, about the way she had been making love— or sex—in a frivolous, and some people might say sordid, way with her best friend's husband. She was being made to think. Most definitely she did not want to think: it was extraordinary, the strength of her instinct *not* to examine that area of her life.

However, examining it, or rather, touching lightly on it, she was able to congratulate herself, or rather, both herself and dear Fred, that never had they in the presence of their spouses enjoyed that most awful of betrayals, enjoyment of their complicity while their said spouses remained oblivious. She could not remember ever, when together, their so much as looking at each other in an invitation to make love, or sex; she was positive they had never once allowed their eyes to signal: these poor fools don't know our secret. For certainly they had never felt like this. They had not ever, not once, made plans to meet alone. They might have fallen into each other's arms the moment the opportunity offered, as if no other behavior was possible to them, but they did not engineer opportunities. And, having arrived in each other's arms, all laughter and pleasure, there was never a feeling of having gone one better than Althea and Henry, of doing them down in any way. And, having separated, they did not think about what had happened, nor consider their partners: it was as if these occasions belonged to another plane altogether. That trivial, or sordid and unimportant; that friendly, good-natured, and entirely enjoyable plane that lay beside, or above, or within these two so satisfactory marriages.

It occurred to Muriel that its nature, its essence, was lack of emotion. Her feeling for Frederick, what Frederick felt for her, was all calm sense and pleasure, with not so much as a twinge of that yearning anguish we call being in love.

And, thinking about it all, as these long sessions with weeping and miserable (enjoyably miserable?) Althea had made her do, she understood, and became determined to hold on to, her belief that her instinct, or compulsion, never to examine, brood, or make emotional profit-and-loss accounts about the sex she had with Frederick was healthy. For as soon as she did put weight on that area, start to measure and weigh, all sorts of sensations hitherto foreign to this relationship began to gabble, gobble, and insist and demand. Guilt, for one.

She came to a conclusion. It was so seditious of any idea held in common by these four and their kind, that she had to look at it, as it were, sideways. It was this: that very likely the falling-in-love with the young doctor was not at all as Althea was seeing it—as anyone was likely to see it—the point was not the periods of making love—love, not sex!—which of course had been all rapture, though muted, inevitably, with their particular brand of wry and civilized understanding, but it was the spilling of emotion afterward, the anguish, the guilt. Emotion was the point. Great emotion had been felt, had been suffered. Althea had suffered, was suffering abominably. Everyone had got it wrong: the real motive for such affairs was the need to suffer the pain and the yearning afterward.

The two marriages continued to grow like trees, sheltering the children who flourished beneath them.

Soon, they had been married fifteen years.

There occurred another crisis, much worse.

Its prelude was this. Due to a set of circumstances not important—Althea had to visit a sick mother and took the children; Henry was away; the Jones children sent to visit a grandmother—Frederick and Muriel spent two weeks alone with each other. Ostensibly, they were in their separate homes, but they were five minutes' drive from each other, and not even in a gossipy, inbred little English town could neighbors see anything wrong in two people being together a lot who were with each other constantly year in and out.

It was a time of relaxation. Of enjoyment. Of quiet. They spent nights in the same bed—for the first time. They took long intimate meals together alone—for the first time. They had seldom been alone together, when they came to think of it. It was extraordinary how communal it was, the life of the Joneses and the Smiths.

Their relationship, instead of being the fleeting, or flighty thing it had been, rolls in the hay (literally), or in the snow, an hour on the drawing-room carpet, or a quick touch-up in a telephone booth, was suddenly all dignity, privacy, and leisure.

And now Frederick showed a disposition to responsible feeling—"love" was the word he insisted on using, while Muriel nervously implored him not to be solemn. He pointed out that he was betraying his beloved Althea, that she was betraying her darling Henry, and that this was what they had been doing for years and years, and without a twinge of guilt of a moment's reluctance.

And without, Muriel pointed out, *feeling*.

Ah, yes, she was right, how awful, he was really beginning to feel that. . . .

For God's sake, she cried, stop it, don't spoil everything, can't you see the dogs of destruction are sniffing at our door?

Stop it, darling Fred, I won't have you using words like love, no, no, that is our redeeming point, our strength—we haven't been in love, we have never agonized over each other, desired each other, missed each other, wanted each other; we have not ever "felt" anything for each other. . . .

Frederick allowed it to be seen that he found this view of them too cool, if not heartless.

But, she pointed out, what they had done was to help each other in every way, to be strong pillars in a foursome, to rejoice at the birth of each other's children, to share ideas and read books recommended by the other. They had enjoyed random and delightful and irresponsible sex without a twang of conscience when they could—had, in short, lived for fifteen years in close harmony.

Fred called her a sensible woman.

During that fortnight love was imminent on at least a dozen occasions. She resisted.

But there was no doubt, and Muriel saw this with an irritation made strong by self-knowledge—for of course she would have adored to be "in love" with Frederick, to anguish and weep and lie awake—that Frederick, by the time his wife came back, was feeling thoroughly deprived. His Muriel had deprived him. Of emotional experience.

Ah, emotion, let us bathe in thee!

For instance, the television, that mirror of us all:

A man has crashed his car, and his wife and three children have burned to death.

"And what did you feel when this happened?" asks the bland, but humanly concerned, young interviewer. "Tell us, what did you *feel*?"

Or, two astronauts have just survived thirty-six hours when every second might have meant their deaths.

"What did you feel? Please tell us, what did you feel?"

Or, a woman's two children have spent all night exposed on a mountaintop but were rescued alive.

"What did you feel?" cries the interviewer. "What did you feel while you were waiting?"

An old woman has been rescued from a burning building by

a passerby, but for some minutes had every reason to think that her end had come.

"What did you feel? You thought your number was up, you said that, didn't you? What did you feel when you thought that?"

What do you think I felt? You silly nit, you jackal, what would you have felt in my place? Doesn't everybody watching this program know perfectly well what I felt? So why ask me when you know already?

Why, madam?—of course it is because feeling is our substitute for tortured slaves and dying gladiators. We have to feel sad, anxious, worried, joyful, agonized, delightful. I feel. You feel. They felt. I felt. We were feeling . . . if we don't feel, then how can we believe that anything is happening to us at all?

And since none of us feel as much as we have been trained to believe that we ought to feel in order to prove ourselves profound and sincere people, then luckily here is the television where we can see other people feeling for us. So tell me, madam, what did you *feel* while you stood there believing that you were going to be burned to death? Meanwhile, the viewers will be chanting our creed: we feel, therefore we are.

Althea came back, the children came back, life went on, and Frederick almost at once fell violently in love with a girl of twenty who had applied to be a receptionist in the surgery. And Muriel felt exactly the same, but on the emotional plane, as a virtuously frigid wife—so we are told—when her husband went to a prostitute: "If I had only given him what he wanted, he wouldn't have gone to *her!*"

For she knew that her Frederick would not have fallen in love with the girl if she had allowed him to be in love with her. He had had an allowance of "love" to be used up, because he had not understood—he had only said that he did—that he was wanting to fall in love: He needed the condition of being in love, needed to feel all that. Or, as Muriel muttered (but only very privately, and to herself), he needed to suffer. She should have allowed him to suffer. It is clear that everybody needs it.

And now there was this crisis, a nasty one, which rocked all four of them. Althea was unhappy, because her marriage was at stake: Frederick was talking of a divorce. And of course she was remembering her lapse with the young doctor four years before, and the living lie she had so ably maintained since. And Frederick was suicidal, because he was not so stupid as not to know that to leave a wife he adored, and was happy with, for the sake of a girl of twenty was—stupid. He was past forty-five. But he had never loved before, he said. He actually said this, and to Henry, who told Muriel.

Henry, who so far had not contributed a crisis, now revealed that he had suffered similarly some years before, but "it had not seemed important." He confessed this to Muriel, who felt some irritation. For one thing, she felt she had never really appreciated Henry as he deserved, because the way he said "it had not seemed important" surely should commend itself to her. Yet it did not; she felt in some ridiculous way belittled because he made light of what had been—surely?— a deep experience. And if it had not, why not? And then, she felt she had been betrayed; that she was able to say to herself she was being absurd did not help. In short, suddenly Muriel was in a bad way. More about Frederick than about Henry. Deprived in a flash of years of sanity, she submerged under waves of jealousy of the young girl, of deprivation—but of what? what? she was in fact deprived of nothing!—of sexual longing, and of emotional loneliness. Her Henry, she had always known, was a cold fish. Their happiness had been a half-thing. Her own potential had always been in cold storage. And so she raged and suffered, for the sake of Frederick, her real love—so she felt now. Her only love. How could she have been so mad as not to enjoy being really in love, two weeks of love. How could she not have seen, all those years, where the truth lay. How could she. . . .

That was what she felt. What she *thought* was, and knew, that she was mad. Everything she felt now had nothing, but nothing to do with her long relationship with Frederick, which was pleasant as a good healthy diet and as unremarkable, and nothing to do with her marriage with Henry, whom she loved deeply, and who made her happy, and whose humorous and civilized company she enjoyed more than anyone's.

Frederick brought his great love to an end. Or, to put it accurately, it was brought to an end: the girl married. For a while he sulked; he could not forgive life for his being nearly fifty. Althea helped him come back to himself, and to their life together.

Muriel and Henry reestablished their loving equilibrium.

Muriel and Frederick for a long time did not, when they found themselves together, make sex. That phase had ended, so they told each other, when they had a discussion: they had never had a discussion of this sort before, and the fact that they were having one seemed proof indeed that they had finished with each other. It happened that this talk was taking place in his car, he having picked her up from some fete given to raise funds for the local hospital. Althea had not been able to attend. The children, once enjoyers of such affairs, were getting too old for them. Muriel was attending on behalf of them all, and Frederick was giving her a lift home. Frederick stopped the car on the edge of a small wood, which was now damp and brown with winter: this desolation seemed a mirror of their own dimmed and aging state. Suddenly, no word having been spoken, they were in an embrace, and shortly thereafter, on top of his coat and under hers in a clump of young birches whose shining winter branches dropped large, tingling, lively drops tasting of wet bark onto their naked cheeks and arms.

But, the psychologically oriented reader will be demanding, what about those children? Adolescent by now, surely?

Quite right. The four had become background figures for the dramas of the young ones' adolescence; their passions were reflections of their children's; and part of their self-knowledge had to be that Frederick's need to be in love and the associated traumas were sparked off by the adults being continually stimulated by their five attractive offspring, all of whom of course perpetually in love or in hate.

It goes without saying, too, that the parents felt even more guilty and inadequate because they worried that their lapses—past, present, and imaginary—might have contributed to the stormy miseries of the children. Which we all know too well to have to go through again—but what violence! what quarrels! what anguish! Adolescence is like this. The Jones and Smith youngsters were behaving exactly as they were expected to. Oh, the dramas and the rebellions, the leavings of home and the sullen returns; oh, the threats of drug-taking, then the drug-taking and the return to caution; the near-pregnancies, the droppings out and in, the ups and downs at schools, the screamed accusations at the parents for their total stupidity, backwardness, thickheadedness, and responsibility for all the ills in the world.

But just as the script prescribes crisis, so it prescribes the end of crisis. Those five attractive young people, with benefits of sound middle-class background and its institutions, with their good education, with their intelligent and concerned parents—what could go wrong? Nothing did. They did well enough at school and were soon to go to the university. Could they have any other future beyond being variations on the theme of their parents?

Twenty years had passed.

There came an opportunity for the two doctors to join a large doctors' combine in London. It was in a working-class area, but the senior doctors had consulting rooms in Harley Street. Doctors Smith and Jones had continued idealistic, conditionally socialist, and were shocked by the thought that they might also succumb to what they thought of as a Jekyll-and-Hyde existence.

The two families decided to buy a very large house in North London, and to divide it. That way they would all have much more space than if they each had a house. And the children were more like brothers and sisters and should not be separated by anything as arbitrary as a move to a new home.

Soon after the move to London, Henry died. There was no reason for him to die in his fifties. He had thought of himself as healthy. But he had always smoked heavily, he was rather plump, and he had always worked very hard. These were reasons enough, it was thought, for him to have a stroke and for Muriel to be a widow in her forties.

Muriel stayed in the shared house with her two children, a boy of eighteen and a girl of fourteen. After discussing it thoroughly with Althea, Frederick made arrangements to help support Muriel, to be a father to the children, to support this other family as he was sure Henry would have done for Althea and the three children if it had been Frederick who had had the stroke. As it might have been: Frederick's habits and constitution were similar to Henry's. Frederick was secretly frightened, made resolutions to eat less, smoke less, work less, worry less: but he was doing more of everything because Henry had gone.

In order to support his greater responsibilities, Frederick attended two days a week and a morning in Harley Street— Muriel acted as his receptionist there, and for the two other doctors who shared his set of rooms. He also worked hard in the combine's clinics, making up by evening sessions and night visiting for time spent in Moneyland. So Frederick and Muriel were now working together, as well as seeing each other constantly in the much-shared family life. Muriel was more with Frederick than Althea was.

And now that Muriel was a widow, and the opportunities were more, the sex life of the two had become as stable as good married sex.

Muriel, thinking about it, had decided that it was probable Frederick had deliberately "stepped up" his sexual life with her because he knew she must be feeling sexually deprived. This was very likely the kind of sexually friendly consideration that would happen in a polygamous marriage. What made her come to this conclusion was that now they would often cuddle as married people do, for instance staying an hour or so after time in the Harley Street rooms, their arms around each other, discussing the day's problems, or perhaps driving off onto Hampstead Heath to discuss the children, sharing warmth and affection—like married people.

For Fred could hardly be missing this sort of affection, far from it, and that he was giving it to her must be the result of a conscious decision, of kindness.

They sometimes did say to each other that what they all had together—but only they two knew it—was a polygamous marriage.

When in company, and people were discussing marriage, the marriage problems of Western man, the problems caused

---

by the emancipation of women, monogamy, fidelity, whether one should "tell" or not, these two tended to remain silent or to make indifferent remarks that sounded in spite of themselves impatient—as people do when entertaining inadmissible thoughts.

Both of them, the man and the woman, had found themselves thinking, had even heard themselves exclaiming aloud as the result of such thoughts: "What a lot of rubbish, what lies!"—meaning, no less, these intelligent and sensible ideas we all do have about the famous Western problematical marriage.

Muriel had only understood that she was married to Frederick when she started to think about marrying again: but it was not likely that anyone would want to marry a forty-five-year-old woman with children at their most demanding and difficult time. She could not imagine marrying again: for it would mean the end of her marriage with Frederick. This was probably how they would all go on, into their old age, or until one of them died.

This was Muriel's thinking on the situation.

Frederick: Muriel was right—he had indeed thought carefully about his old friend's loneliness. She would probably not marry again. She was not, after all, of the generation where there were more men than women. And there was something too independent and touch-me-not about her. Her silences were challenging. Her green eyes were frank. A tall, rangy woman with bronze hair—she dyed it—people noticed her, and called her beautiful or striking: of her, people used the strong adjectives. The older she got, the dryer and cooler became her way of talking. Enemies called her unkind, or masculine; friends, witty. *He* enjoyed these qualities, but would he if they were not the other half, as it were, of Althea? Whom people tended to call "little." So did he. Dear little Althea.

He would give Muriel as much warmth, as much sex as he could, without, of course, giving any less to his wife. For years his relations with Muriel had been all jam, nothing to pay, a bonus. Now he felt her as part of his sudden increase in responsibility when Henry died, part of what he must give to the two children. He was fond of Muriel—indeed, he was sure he loved her. He knew he loved the children almost as well as his own. It was an ungrudging giving of himself—but there was something else in him, another worm was at work. For what was strongest in Frederick now neither his wife nor Muriel knew anything about. It was his longing for the girl Frances—now married with children. Neither of his women had understood how deep that had gone. He had not understood it himself at the time.

Now, years later, it seemed to him that his life was divided between dark, or perhaps a clear flat gray, and light—Frances. Between everything heavy, plodding, difficult, and everything delicious—Frances. Nothing in his actual life fed delight or sprang from it: somewhere else was a sweetness and ease which he had known once, when he had loved Frances.

By now he did know that Frances, a lovely but quite ordinary girl, must be a stand-in for something else. It must be so. No small human being could possibly support the weight of such a force and a fierceness of longing, of want, of need. From time to time, when he straightened himself morally, and physically—for it was like a physical anguish, from a pain that swept all through him, or when he woke up in the morning, out of a dream that was all pain of loss, to see Althea's sleeping face a few inches away on the other pillow, he had to tell himself this: It is not possible that I am suffering all this, year after year, because of a girl I was in love with for a few crazy months.

Yet that was how it felt. On one side was the life he actually led; on the other, ''Frances.''

His intelligence told him everything it ought, such as that if he had been fool enough to leave Althea for Frances, or if Frances had been fool enough to marry him, that in a very short time Frances would have been a dear, known face on a shared pillow, and that what Frances had represented would have moved its quarters elsewhere.

But that was not what he felt. Although he worked so hard—it was virtually two jobs that he had now, one with the poor and the ignorant, for whom he remained concerned, and one with the rich—although he maintained with the most tender love and consideration the emotional and physical needs of the two women; although he was a good and tactful father for five children—he felt he had nothing, lacked everything.

Althea: we move into the shoes, or behind the eyes, of the innocent party.

These three people had all taken on loads with the death of Henry. With Muriel working, Althea's was to run all the large house, to do the shopping, to cook, to be always available for the children. She did not mind it; she had never wanted a career. But it was hard work, and soon she felt herself to be all drudgery and domesticity, and just at the time when, with the children older, she had looked forward to less. But this strain was nothing compared to the real one, which was that she had cared very much about being so attractive, and cherished for it. Cherished no less, she demanded even more of her vanishing looks. She could not bear to think that soon she would be elderly, soon Frederick would not want her. Comparing her tragic sessions in front of her mirror, and her feelings of inadequacy, with her husband's affection, she knew that she was unreasonable. Well, it was probably the "change."

She read many medical books and consulted another doctor—not one her husband knew—and got pills and came to regard her emotional state, all of it, everything she thought and felt, as a symptom without validity.

For she knew that her relationship with her husband was warm, good—wonderful. While other people's marriages frayed and cracked and fell apart, hers, she knew, was solid.

But when she looked at her life, when she looked back, she, too, divided what she saw into two. For her, the sunlit time lay on the other side of the affair with the young doctor. It was not the physical thing she regretted, no; it was that she had not told her husband. Time had done nothing at all to soften her guilt about it. Frederick and she had known a time of perfection, of complete trust and belief. Then she, Althea, had chosen to destroy it. It was her fault that he had fallen so much in love with the girl Frances. Oh, he was likely to fall in love with someone at some point—of course, everyone did, hadn't she? But so violently? That could only have been because of some deep lack between them. And she knew what it was: she had told him lies, had not trusted him.

She was left now with much more than she deserved. If she had to share him now—a little, with Muriel, then it was what she deserved. Besides, if she, Althea, had been left a widow, then she would have leaned as heavily on Henry. On who else?

Sometimes Althea had wild moments when she decided to tell Frederick about the young doctor; but that would be absurd, out of proportion. To talk about it now would surely be to destroy what they still had. To say: For more than a decade now I have been lying to you—she could not imagine herself actually doing it.

Sometimes she listened to other people talking about their marriages, and it seemed to her that they were able to take infidelities much more lightly. Lies, too. Althea kept telling herself that there was something very wrong in her, that she kept brooding about it, worrying, grieving.

For instance, there were these people who went in for wife-swapping. They thought nothing of making love in heaps and in bunches, all together. Some of them said their marriages were strengthened—perhaps they were. Perhaps if she and her Fred had shared each other with other couples . . . who, Muriel and Henry?—no, surely that could be too dangerous, too close? Surely they—the wife-swappers—made a rule not to get involved too close to home? But that was not the point at all, the point was the lying, the deception.

The fact was, the only person in the world who knew all the truth about her was Muriel. Muriel had known about the young doctor, and knew about the years of lying. How odd that was, for your woman friend to be closer than your own husband! It was *intolerable*. Unbearable. Althea found it horrible to say to herself: I trust Muriel more than I do Frederick; my behavior has proved that I do.

Of course she had sometimes had her thoughts about Frederick and Muriel. She had recently been jealous—a little, not much. This was because Muriel was working with Frederick now.

Often, when the three of them were together, Althea would

look at those two, her husband, her closest friend, and think: Of course, if I died, they would marry. This was not envy, but her way of coming to terms with it. She even thought—though this was the sort of thing Muriel said, the kind of thing people expected from Muriel: This is a sort of group marriage, I suppose.

But Althea did not suspect a sexual tie. Not that he hadn't often said he found Muriel attractive. But one always could sense that sort of thing. Of course in all those years there must have been something: a kiss or two? A little more, perhaps, after a party or something like that? But not much more; these two would never deceive her. She could trust Muriel with anything; her old friend was a well into which confidences vanished and were forgotten; Muriel never gossiped, never condemned. She was the soul—if one could use that old-fashioned word—of humor. As for Frederick, when he had fallen in love, not only his wife, but the whole world had known of it: he was not a man who could, or who wanted to, conceal his feelings. But the real thing was this: the three of them had made, and now lived inside, an edifice of kindliness and responsibility and decency; it was simply not possible that this could harbor deception. It was inconceivable. So much so that Althea did not think about it: it was not sexual jealousy that she felt.

But she felt something else that she was ashamed of, that she had to wrestle with, in silence and in secrecy. It was this: she could not stop herself thinking that if Henry could die without warning, apparently in full health, then why not Frederick?

Althea was by nature a fussy and attentive wife, but Frederick did not like this in her. She longed to say: Take it easy, work less, worry less—relax. She knew he believed that he ought to be doing all this; duty ordained otherwise.

Often she would wake in the night out of dreams full of terror: if Frederick was on call, she would see the bed empty beside her, and think that this was what she could expect from the future. Then she would go to the stairs to see if Muriel's light was still on: it often was, and then Althea would descend the stairs to Muriel's kitchen, where they would drink tea or cocoa until Frederick came back. Muriel did not ask what drove Althea down the stairs so often at night, but she was always gay and consoling—kind. She was kind. Well, they were all kind people.

Sometimes, on those rare evenings when they could all be together, without pressures from Frederick's work, Althea, having cleared the table and come to join those two people, her husband—a large worried-looking man in spectacles sitting by a lamp and piles of medical magazines, engaged in his futile task of keeping up with each new discovery—and a lean, rather restless, woman who was probably helping one of the youngsters with homework, or a psychological problem— sometimes Althea would see that room without its center, without Frederick. She and Muriel were alone in the room with the children. Yes, that is how it would all end, two aging women, with the children—who would soon have grown up and gone. Between one blink of an eye and another, a man could vanish, as Henry had done.

In the long evenings when Frederick was at the clinic, or on call, and it was as if the whole house and its occupants waited for him to come back, then Althea could not stop herself from looking across the living room at Muriel with the thought: *Coming events cast their shadow before. Can't you feel it?*

But Muriel would look up, smile, laugh, offer to make tea for them all, or would say that she heard Frederick's car and she was tired and would take herself to bed—for she was tactful, and never stayed on in the evenings past the time she was wanted.

But this is our future, Althea would think. Their future, hers and Muriel's, was each other.

She knew it. But it was neurotic to think like this and she must try to suppress it.

Barbara Grizzuti Harrison

SEXUAL CHIC, SEXUAL FASCISM AND SEXUAL CONFUSION

Sometimes, in my more sourly pessimistic, I-think-the-world-is-broken moods, I find myself ready to believe that New York's sexual avant-garde may be entering the era of the closet heterosexual. Only a couple of years ago, I, like all feminists, found myself called upon to explain to every dim-witted or threatened antagonist that, no, we weren't all lesbians. It was tedious and enervating to have to do so, and it was usually a waste of time; but it wasn't scary. After all, one was standing on firm ground—the ground of one's own necessities. I, for example, knew damn well that I was heterosexual—in spite of my having had a clumsy grope with my friend Rosie when I was twelve years old. Of course I could *imagine* a woman pleasuring me sexually—anybody with two hands and a mouth can pleasure anybody else; but I couldn't, without laughing, conceive of kissing a woman passionately, or cuddling with a woman. I couldn't imagine experiencing with a woman the delight and abandon, the desire for a union that transcends differences, the pleasures of symmetry and otherness that come with loving a man.

While it is true that for me, as for most of the women I know, encounters with men have more often than not been full of pain and defeat, it is also true that they've been full of the kind of joy—and fun—I have not been able to imagine sharing with a woman.

But times have changed. Recently I answered my phone four times to hear four heterosexual female friends saying, "You'll never guess what happened." After the third time, I didn't have to guess: they had all been to bed with women. And many of the feminists who not too long ago were scrupulously asserting their immutable heterosexuality are now grieving because they have not found themselves able to go to bed with women. The question that vexes them is, "If we really love women, why don't we go to bed with them?" And I find that scary, largely because no logical answer immediately presents itself—"I don't want to" just sounds petulant and shallow.

Nowadays, when a lot of women are flirting with what Simone de Beauvoir calls "the miracle of the mirror," the sentiments expressed by writer Sheila Charas begin to seem almost anachronistic. "Women are nice people," Charas says, "—and there's not a woman in the world who has the power to move me the way a man I love has. I expect women to 'understand' me—as casually as I expect a mirror to give back my own reflection. It's easy to be frank and free and fully myself with women, because we speak the same language, we recognize our common cause, we're the same person. But I can't proceed from those abstractions to a love affair with a woman. Perhaps because I'm convinced that for a man really to know me is an epiphany. Or maybe it's because the communication women have with each other is not all it's cracked up to be: we exchange information about a common situation; we don't really take imaginative leaps into each other's consciousness. As far as I'm concerned, women who love women can have the harmony; I'll take the counterpoint."

But what about women who are choosing "the harmony"? Are they "proceeding from abstractions" into bed? Do they conceive of homosexual love affairs as a correct expression of their political beliefs? Or—horrible thought—is it that to be "sensually mobile," to have it off with anyone who comes along, to be casually bisexual, is now not only permissible, but chic? A Marxist friend suggests an even more horrible thought. Polymorphous sex, he says, is the ruling class's idea of a great new consumer commodity: "After all, if you have a husband in Florida, a male lover in Boston, and a female lover in New York, you have to have plenty of money for plane fare. . . . And you don't have much energy for anything else. If sex is the revolution, there *is* no revolution." And what, lest we forget, has love to do with it all?

Trying to find the answers to these questions is sometimes a little like taking a walk through Cloud Cuckoo Land. For one thing, watching women bludgeon and contort themselves into the "politically appropriate" sexual behavior and emotional responses can be pretty dispiriting.

Take, for example, this story, told to me by Margaret Sloan, a contributing editor at *Ms.* and an avowed lesbian. A group of feminists picketing Hugh Hefner's Chicago Playboy Club released a statement to the press declaring that they were all lesbians. In point of fact, they were not. They were *political* lesbians—straight women who, "in order to share the oppression of their sisters" and to forgo "male privilege," had chosen . . . oh well, why go on? I suppose they made at least as much sense as the young *white* men who carried signs during Vietnam protest marches declaring "No Vietnamese ever called me nigger."

Sloan was, justifiably, full of anger for "those tacky women who go into gay bars, play with your sexuality and your emotions . . . and then go home to a man. Sometimes they even come to bars with men to protect them while they flirt. What kind of thing is that to do, with lonely lesbians all around?" But Sloan didn't seem quite sure what attitude to strike in regard to political lesbians. On the one hand, she seemed eager to guard her turf: "They mess up the rest of us who are into the whole life-style. They mock people who've made a real personal and emotional choice." On the other hand, she felt obliged to remark that, man being the "enemy," "we need all the help we can get."

A lot of help seems to be forthcoming. Dr. Jean Mundy, a psychologist who estimates that one third of her patients are gay women, said she knew "many very beautiful women intimately connected with men—some of them married," who were, because of "identification with the oppressed," declaring themselves to be lesbians. When I told Dr. Mundy that if I were living with a heterosexual man who made a gratuitous proclamation of homosexuality I would consider it not a political statement but a muddy lie, an affront, an abandonment, and a rejection for which I would cheerfully kill him, she looked at me, I thought, as if I were a dinosaur.

And when I told her that I thought the comic/grotesque elements of sex would, in the absence of lust, abandon, or passion, make any homosexual coupling impossible for me, she suggested that my feeling was the result of having been "trained to believe women are inferior and second class . . . perhaps you feel as if you'd be making love to a slave or an animal." I protested that I really didn't think I regarded women either as slaves or as animals, but Dr. Mundy wasn't impressed.

Nevertheless, a lot of sensitive, intelligent women are questioning their "bent" for heterosexuality, with more than a little help from their friends.

Barbara Seaman (author of *Free and Female*), for example, told me that she used to "fall all over myself explaining to frightened women that we weren't all lesbians." Now she exhorts women on the lecture circuit not to "knock it unless you've tried it." Barbara hasn't tried it; but she's more or less persuaded that she *ought* to like it: "I'm reluctant to write about sex now . . . I feel my experience is so limited . . . so many women are becoming omnisexual. They're more courageous than I am. . . . I trust women. There's always that terrible fear of being abandoned by a man . . . but then, when he leaves, you can always tell yourself, 'What does he know? He's only a man.' If a woman were to abandon me, I don't know what I would do. . . . I used to feel a lot of fear and contempt coming from straight women about lesbians. Now the question I'm hearing from a lot of my friends is 'Why *can't* we be like them?'"

Having now talked to about a dozen women who are having homosexual affairs, I learned that my own feelings about these women had very little to do with whose head (or heads) they preferred to have on the pillow next to theirs. I found some women who were loving and generous and good, and some who were a pain in the neck; some who were pleasant and some who were dreary; some who seemed to be acting out of profound visceral and emotional feelings, and some who wouldn't recognize their feelings if they were put in a suitcase and deposited on their doorstep; and some whose

Barbara Grizzuti Harrison

conversation was such an incredible pastiche of dimly perceived emotion and half-baked ideology, rhetoric, and gut-spill that I doubt if anyone, themselves included, could make any sense of, or see any pattern in, what they were doing. Still, the reasons people give for what they do are generally pretty instructive:

Dorothy (not her real name) is a magazine editor and a feminist activist. She is tough-minded, shy, eager to like and be liked, empathetic, sharp-witted, self-mocking, and full of acknowledged contradictions; she gives the impression of total vulnerability. Two years ago her marriage of eight years broke up, leaving her with a young daughter and too many empty nights.

"I've never had one-night stands," Dorothy says, "I'm not an accumulator of sexual experience. I'm not putting it down—there are women I respect who have gratifying, brief experiences with men or women (usually when they're in another town) and then come home to a solid heterosexual relationship; I'm just not up to that.

"After two years in a consciousness-raising group—with twelve white, heterosexual, middle-class, overeducated women (just like me)—I began to acknowledge to myself that I could have sexual feelings for women. I was scared to talk about it, but not talking about it made me feel crazy and fragmented. Here was all this intense friendship and affection and emotional liability—and no sex. When I did start to open up to the idea, I resisted it by thinking, Why spoil a relationship with a woman by having sex? As soon as sex enters the picture, there's manipulation, passivity, aggression, sadism, masochism. . . . I had an overwhelming fear that I'd duplicate all that horrible stuff in a relationship with a woman. Then something happened that made my dithering irrelevant: I fell in love with a woman. It felt exactly like an intense relationship I had had with an older woman in my teens . . . a manipulative woman, I might add, who used sex to tantalize and titillate me, even though it was not an overtly sexual relationship. I was as intoxicated and infatuated as I had been then. And you know what? It was exactly like the early stages of being in love with a man. I invested her with superiority. I felt suffocated by my feelings. I was looking for clues, as I do with a man—did she or didn't she want to? Finally I asked her, yes or no? She said no. She was afraid that if she ever slept with a woman it would totally sever her connection with men. (That didn't stop her from being seductive with women, of course.)

"After that, I almost immediately went to bed with a radical lesbian; I just had to know what it was like—what it was like physically, I mean. And physically—technically—it was good. But what does 'good' mean? When I conceived my child, that was good, too—lyrical. I can't really measure pleasure in terms of orgasms. It didn't feel like a union, it didn't have the intensity of coital movements. The thing is— and that experience proved it to me—I can have casual sex with a woman, sex on the level of physical satisfaction, period. I've never been able to have casual sex with a man.

"So sex with this woman was 'good.' But, Jesus, I felt like she was swallowing me up in politics. Suddenly Jill Johnston was in my life, in my apartment. There were militant lesbians tramping in and out of the place, I was a political prize. I had professional credibility and visibility in the feminist world, and they saw me as a tool in the lesbian struggle. I was being pressured to make a commitment to lesbian identity, and I felt exploited. I couldn't stand the *life*. I don't want to make love to a textbook of ideology. I resist being identified by my bed partner. We're more than projectiles and orifices, after all. And in any case, how could I honestly know what it is to feel like a lesbian? I'm still interested in men."

I asked Dorothy, who has now had three brief affairs with women, if "all that horrible stuff" that happens with men was in fact duplicated in her relationships with women: "It sure was. I dream of egalitarian love, a love of peers. I knew it was going to be hard to find it with a man. If I'm thinking I'm his equal, and he's thinking he's my superior, what chance do we have? Wouldn't you think a relationship between equals would mean the end of role-playing? Well, I've seen women turn other women into wives and housekeepers. I've seen role-playing like you wouldn't believe—straight from Central Casting. . . . The heavy lesbian political line makes *sense*. It's *logical*—but it doesn't seem to have anything to do with the way people really feel and behave . . . falling in love *happens,* romantic tension *happens.* . . . And I don't want to be hit over the head with ideology.''

Could it happen again for her with a man? "I don't want to shut myself off from the possibility of going to bed with men," she said. "I just want a good relationship—I seek out a person, not an experience. I don't want to live in a world of Amazons. I just want somebody to love me.''

Only a cynic could regard Dorothy as a greedy sexual "consumer"; and this nice, muddled, unhappy person is about as chic as Fanny Farmer. De Beauvoir's words about homosexual relationships seem to apply in Dorothy's case. They are "one way, among others, in which a woman solves the problem posed by her condition in general, her erotic situation in particular.'' But what Dorothy has found, in attempting this particular solution, is that "*every* human relationship implies conflict.'' While she is adamant that "homosexual experience doesn't define me as perverse or aberrant,'' she certainly doesn't qualify for a chapter in *Lesbian True Romances.* "In all my lesbian affairs,'' she says, "our mutual grief and pain was the basis of the relationship. I shared my most intimate pain before I even knew whether my lover and I could enjoy the same movie. . . . It was never lighthearted. It was a feast of sorrows.''

Most of the women I know describe their homosexual relationships modestly. Sally (a pseudonym), for example. She is 32, beautiful by any standard except, perhaps, her own. A rounded size 12, she lives from crash diet to crash diet, convinced no man will ever love her if she's "fat." In the ten years I've known her, Sally has seldom been without a man. For Sally, beauty is a prerequisite in a man; since her divorce, most of her men—many of whom she meets in SoHo bars— have been younger than she, pretty, and narcissistic. In the past year, she has been to bed four times with a woman, although she says, "The first time a woman made an overture to me, I hit her.''

Sally is not a feminist but, she says, "The women's movement was critical in that it allowed me to express my feelings for women. I knew other women were trying things, so it didn't seem so weird and far out. And how can you live in New York and have friends and go to bars and know everybody's doing it and not want to try it yourself? I wish I could say the movement has helped me to be less silly and less needy with men. It hasn't—but it's released my feelings for women.

"It started when I went to bed with my friend Erica and two men. I had good sex with the men, and practically nothing with Erica, apart from an occasional touch, which put me really uptight. But I woke up in the morning not giving a damn about the men, and loving Erica and knowing she'd *be there* for me. After that it was easy to go to bed with a woman—I liked being close to women, it was lovely to be able to put my arms around a woman and kiss her, but I never thought I could let myself get into genital sex. Women don't turn me on that way. The thought of a woman does nothing for me. But in bed with women, I have warm loving feelings. The most fantastic sexual experience of my life was going to bed with my friend Linda and a guy we both really liked. A whole *lot* of things happened—including genital—it was fantastic. . . . I hate being overweight. Linda's overweight too, she's no more perfect than I am, but I loved her smooth, full, womanly body. It made me like myself better—in a way that no man has ever made me like myself. I liked my body through her body."

Sally has never been to bed with a woman alone. Could she? "No, basically I'm turned on by men. I couldn't have gone to bed with Linda if a man hadn't been there. If I had to make a desert island one-and-only choice, it would be the missionary position forever. I'm turned on by men I don't even *like*. I have lust for men and love for women. I haven't any free-floating sexual curiousity about women. I made random love to men who don't care, who don't matter. I couldn't pick up a woman for sex. All my strong loyalties are with women. When I need comfort and understanding, I go to a woman;

there isn't a single man I can call in the middle of the night. I keep hoping to find lust and love in the same place—in a man."

Linda, who was sitting with us, turned to me and said: "Doesn't it worry you that you won't risk your heterosexuality by going to bed with women? The reason I can do it is that I know I'm basically heterosexual. I know that I'm not going to get addicted. But why are *you* threatened?"

The Jesuitical accusation that I was less heterosexual than women who were "secure" enough to go to bed with other women was one I was to hear over and over again. That, and the bland invitation to "try it—you'll like it" (as if I were a recalcitrant child stupidly spurning a dish of caviar), and the implication that not to assert one's "natural" bisexuality amounted to a hang-up so heavy as to be a moral defect.

When I arranged to meet her, Wendy (another pseudonym) said I'd be sure to recognize her because she was the "plain mousy one." A prominent social psychologist in her early thirties, she certainly does not suggest ripe sexuality . . . and indeed she says she is "seldom overcome by passion." Nevertheless, Wendy finds time for three "committed relationships": a husband, who lives in Georgia, whom she sees about once a month ("I can't imagine my life without him: I like to talk to him about ideas and about the way the world is, we do a kind of Mutt and Jeff act, it's fun"); a male live-in lover—a graphic designer with whom she has a "nonverbal, very sexual relationship . . . we share a visual awareness"; and a female lover in Pittsburgh, with whom she has "a very flirtatious, emotional, affectionate relationship." All these people, Wendy says, are "gentle, adrogynous, sensual." All have, at one time or another, been to bed with one another: "We all like one another a lot."

Because Wendy frequently appears on panels discussing alternate life-styles, she is "often asked by straight women to take them on. . . . I guess I'm sort of an advertisement of how good sex with women can be. But I always tell them, no. I don't want the responsibility for somebody's first try. My own first experience was easy: I was writing a book on sexuality with another woman, and we said, why not just *do* it? So we did it. It was good. Women provide immediate gratification. Most men don't know how to do it. They don't pick up on your cues, they're really not interested. So you lie and tell them it was good, and then you have contempt for them because they've believed your lies."

Does she, then, like women more than men? "When I was a young teenager, I was in love with an extraordinarily attractive older woman—a kind of Miss Jean Brodie type. Through her I came to believe that women were the creators of poetry— women could combine the best qualities of earth mother and intellectual—and men were uninteresting. . . . Now, though, I'm not even sure if men in general are different from women. I don't like *macho* men or *macho* women. I look for a person, not a gender. I go to my lovers for the different personalities they allow me to express, and I relate to them in the same way I look for commonality, and I'm interested in differences. I don't feel men are intimidating or unknowable; both men and women are equally secret and not secret, equally predictable and not predictable. Probably the men I love are more like women than like the average American male."

Well, but what about the romantic idea of finding everything in one person, of having one person to hold you against the dark? Does Wendy ever feel the need to be loved/held/ known/comforted by one person only, one person alone? She doesn't; she doesn't want a lover to be "the corner I hide in." Wendy believes she's found a way to have both autonomy and intimacy: "As much as possible I want to be there for the people I love—all of them. No one can be there all the time. I don't expect it. I don't demand it. I don't take people on. I'm not responsible for their happiness. I don't want relationships where I'm the whole social-emotional link with the world. I'm interested in my lovers for the things they add to me."

While Wendy credits the women's movement with rein- forcing ideas that she has always had—"it validated my belief that women could be autonomous, independent, strong, lov- ing; I've found a group of people who will support me in what the straight world considers my 'craziness'"—she is furious with the "fascistic Calvinistic lesbians who put bisexuality down. They're always telling me I'll turn to men in the crunch. What the hell is 'the crunch,' and why should they assume I'd turn to men unless *they* believe men have superior claims? They corner me at parties with their tirades. All that stuff— about 'male privilege' and so on—is irrelevant to me."

Dorothy, Sally, and Wendy are representative of the dozen or so bisexual women I spoke with who are ready to take their chances with men or with women. If there is a pattern, a simple magical explanation for why they are able to turn to women while others of us are not, I fail to discern it. Many women who can't, won't, or haven't yet made love to women express terrible fears of being abandoned and rejected by the women they love. (Alix Shulman, the author of *Memoirs of an Ex-Prom Queen,* says she can imagine no worse pain than being abandoned by a sister.) But lesbians like Margaret Sloan say the same thing: "I have never risked so much with a man. I hurt more when a woman hurts me; I'm just wiped out, because I trust women." Almost all the women I spoke with— with the exception of Wendy, who says she has it all—are needy and want more than they have; but of whom can that not be said? Almost all of the women expressed a preference for "gentle" men (but, on the other hand, some lesbians like a tough, *macho* woman). Every one of them had had a bit of roll-and-tickle with another little girl when she was a kid; but so, according to Kinsey, has about seven-eighths of the adult female population. (And it's worth noting, as Dr. Elayne Kahn of the New York Center for Sexual Guidance points out, that every woman's primal sexual association is with a woman— her mother.) Even if one were to say that lesbians—as opposed to bisexuals or women who have occasional homosexual affairs—"hate" or "reject" men, one would be obliged to say also that many heterosexual women regard men as an unpleasant necessity.

Looking for similarities among women who were having affairs with women, I found mostly differences. There were women who said, "A woman knows your body as well as her own . . . she knows just what to do"; and women who said,

"They're just like men . . . you have to tell them what to do." I found women who had said, "What the hell, let's just do it"; and women who went through a lot of Sturm-und-Drang I WANT YOU hokey stuff before they could do it. There were women who could have casual affairs with men, but only soulful, "meaningful relationships" with women; and other women who could use women casually to satisfy them but needed a man to feel whole and fulfilled. I spoke to women who had done it for the certitude of being able to say, "Now I know I'm not a lesbian"; and women who, once having tried it, felt that they could keep on doing it without sacrificing their heterosexual identity. There were woman who could relate to only one person—male or female—at a time, and women who could take on armies.

What makes it all so confusing is that, while homosexual acts may spring from necessity, they are being justified by ideology. The personal gets lost in the rhetorical. As a lesbian friend of mine says, "Accepting your homosexual inclinations is harder than people would have you think. From the time I was an adolescent I was fascinated by lesbianism. The parts of porn books that got most dog-eared were the parts where women are doing stuff. But I had to learn to look at it politi-cally . . . it was less threatening. If you couch your homosex-uality in ideological terms, you feel you're making it accepta-ble to movement people, and to people who want to be 'with it.'"

But is it true that many lesbians are using ideology to batter straight women into homosexual conformity? "Lesbians," my friend says, "have always been oppressed by straights. How could they not turn around and oppress other people? We're no better than other victims. . . . When we were told that we were not only dangerous to the movement, we were irrele-vant, a lot of us set out to prove that all women had the potential for homosexuality. . . . Who can stand being called irrelevant?" She acknowledges the element of chic in women-with-women, but says, "Some people can't do anything unless it's chic. It was chic to support the Panthers and chic to vote for McGovern."

"If women who love women carried their thinking to its logical conclusion," one lesbian said to me, "they'd *have* to become homosexuals." Maybe so; but maybe, as a theologian I know says, "Every argument carried to its logical conclusion, is absurd—unless it's holy." When logic leads one to violate one's own nature and ways, experience and childhood, when it causes people to give political answers to the intimate questions human beings ask one another, when it is used to coerce women into ways that are not their own, it is indeed absurd.

I think it is patently absurd, for example, to say, as one woman said to me, "I am in a totally satisfying homosexual relationship. But now I'm questioning whether monogamy isn't a male ploy to keep women in their place. So I feel—in spite of my needs for comfort and security—that I must, to make the right political choice, seek an alternate living relationship."

That's where "logic," pushed to its extremities, gets you. It's absurd; but it isn't funny. And just in case there are men around who are laughing, and too eager to put women down for sexual chic, sexual fascism, or homosexual necessity, here is De Beauvoir to remind them of *their* responsibility: "On the day when it will be possible for woman to love, not in her weakness but in her strength, not to escape herself but to find herself, not to abase herself but to assert herself—on that day love will become for her, as for man, a source of life and not of mortal danger. . . . When we abolish the slavery of half of humanity, together with the whole system of hypocrisy that it implies, then the 'division' of humanity will reveal its genuine significance and the human couple will find its true form."

Meanwhile—hard times. Except for those rare people who always seem to make the world work for them, practically every woman I know is either embattled or confused—and a lot of the women I know are bordering on despair. When people feel like that, they're peculiarly susceptible to ideological panaceas and prone to psychic upheavals—and they tend to find comfort, and escape, where they can. Presumably, when—*if*—the happy day De Beauvoir envisions arrives, there will still be women who prefer homosexual love; but let's hope we'll all then be able to be with our freely chosen partners without having to make a political song and dance about it. It's something to look forward to.

At the National Organization for Women's recent conference on marriage and divorce life-styles, fifteen women participated in a panel devoted to an exploration of lesbianism and bisexuality. Of the fifteen, only three had, in fact, had homosexual relationships that precipitated their divorces; the other twelve felt that they "should" be having—or should feel free to explore having—homosexual relationships, without their men's inhibiting them. While several women expressed the fear of being labeled "seekers of the second thrill," the concern of the majority seemed to be how best to approach other women sexually without scaring them off. One recently divorced woman in her mid-forties said that she "loved" her husband and "loved" sex with him—but felt cheated because she was precluded from having "loving relationships" with women. Another woman said that what she had interpreted as competitiveness with and jealousy for other women was in fact disguised sexual love.

When Joyce Snyder, an officer of New York NOW, was asked whether this meeting was symptomatic of gay women exerting "undue political or psychological influence" on the women's movement, she reacted with understandable irritation: "I haven't the vaguest idea," she said, "What's 'undue'? The whole issue of lesbian clout is manufactured by the media because it's juicy—it makes good copy. All women in this movement have their own life-styles and what they bring to the movement is what is important to them. Single women with children have *their* priorities, women who are discriminated against by employers have *their* priorities, dependent married women have *their* priorities—everybody's vocal about what's bothering *her*. Of course lesbians are angry, and noisily angry; they're discriminated against because they're women *and* because they're lesbians. I don't feel lesbians express themselves out of proportion to their numbers, if that's what you mean." Reminded that Betty Friedan had once referred to the lesbian issue as a "lavender herring," and *not* a political issue—thereby arousing great ire among militant gay women—Snyder said, adamantly, that lesbians "presented no organizational problems for NOW. We've moved away from that kind of infighting."

Lesbians themselves seem to be of two minds about whether they are given accurate or sufficient representation in feminist publications. *Ms.*, because of its commercial success, is a frequent target for lesbians' anger—as witness the "Letters to the Editors" column: in a recent issue a lesbian collective criticized the editors for failing to include articles "relevant to lesbians." In the succeeding issue, however, a lesbian wrote in response, "I believe the quickest way to dilute *Ms.* so that it fails all of us is to make it a piecemeal publication of parts aimed at groups." As one beleaguered *Ms.* editor pointed out, "We get into sticky editorial problems. If we commission an article on the phenomenon of women going out with younger men, are we obliged to include the lesbian point of view? *How?* Do we write about older lesbians going out with younger lesbians? Suppose we commission a heterosexual woman to write a piece on sexual jealousy. It's bound to be subjective, right? Is it fair to ask her to write about homosexual jealousy as well as heterosexual jealousy? We see *Ms.* as a magazine for all women—but we never seem to do enough to disarm our critics."

What all this seems to amount to is that anybody who communicates the feminist message through the media is committed to present all aspects of feminism—including bi-sexuality and lesbianism—which is very different from saying that the militant gays dominate the women's movement. There is a lot of gossip about lesbians "taking over" at feminist parties and "coercing" straight women into dancing with them; and many sober (and fair-minded) observers of the women's movement (such as Eve Merriam and Carolyn Heil-brun) have expressed fears that we may—at least in New York City—be headed for a period of rigid separatism between gay feminists and straight feminists. But while proselytizing gays may make a lot of noise, the extent of their psychological impact on the movement is as hard to measure as it is difficult to determine how many kids "copy" TV violence or how many readers of pornography are inspired to rape women—or, for that matter, how many heterosexual women model their love affairs on ideas of romantic love derived from *Cosmopolitan,* John Donne, *Ladies' Home Journal,* or Spencer Tracy and Katharine Hepburn.

Michael Weiss
DIARY OF A MAD HOUSEHUSBAND

Last summer I stayed home and did the housework, watched after the kid, cooked the meals, and silently clucked over the unseeing slobs I lived with. Nobody had suggested that I do the housework, although everybody else was working. I was staying home to write but I wasn't getting anything done and my inactivity was generating a bucketful of anxious energy. I began to look after the house in my own compulsive way. (My mother raised me in a house with a smudge-free glass table. I remember no complaints if we smudged the table, but vaguely recall her in constant motion, an effort so entirely integrated into her life that I sense it more than recall its image.) Nobody seemed to expect me to do it. I became a househusband because I wanted to keep occupied while I was home during the day with just my guilt about not writing and my kid to keep my company. What happened after a while is that my mind began to rot away as I became absorbed in the endless, tedious chores, every one of which was an escape from confronting myself.

In the morning, my wife would kiss me goodbye before I was fully awake and then I would hear the car start and she and the others would be gone to work. My stomach would begin to knot up then and whatever restfulness I had been feeling would fade away. But because it was still early and there was no reason to get out of bed besides the growing fretfulness in my mind and stomach that it was *time to start the day*, I would back toward a restless near-sleep. In the next bedroom I could hear just enough cartoon noises to know that my kid was up and probably sitting next to an empty cereal bowl. On many mornings the phone would ring while I was still in bed—it always seemed to happen just as I slipped back into sleep—but usually it was a business call for my wife. The shades were still drawn and the air conditioner was running.

The gray light and the artificial chill made me more anxious about getting out of bed and facing the day. Finally I would get up, say good morning to my kid, and send him out to play with his friends. Then I could begin my day alone. While I pissed, showered, and brushed my teeth, I also began to clean the bathroom, picking up the wet towels, washing the toothpaste and hair out of the sink and on some mornings scrubbing the tub or the toilet bowl. Then I got dressed, straightened the bedroom, and went downstairs to the first floor. Usually I left behind a shambles in my kid's room, but I had decided (for the first time) that he should be able to keep his room however he wanted.

In the kitchen I began to boil water for tea. While I waited I washed the previous night's supper dishes. Usually I didn't finish cleaning the kitchen during this first encounter. I would take my tea and go into the living room, but before I settled down to read I would begin to straighten up the mess we had left behind the night before. I wanted to read because my mind was being wiped clean of some of what it usually held, like the big ashtray I was emptying of butts in the kitchen garbage bag. Somehow I was back in the kitchen. I bundled up the garbage and took it outside to be collected. Then I went back to the living room and picked up my book and read for a while before I became thirsty. On my way to get a drink I carried the breakfast dishes that everybody else had left on the table into the sink. Then I got a sponge and wiped the table free of crumbs, and got the broom and swept the floor. Before I was finished sweeping I had done the entire downstairs, and when I couldn't find the dustpan I ran upstairs to look for it and ended up sweeping the upstairs too. I was back in the living room before I remembered that I was thirsty. It was nearly noon.

My kid came in for lunch with some friends, and while I made it and cleaned up after them I also made a pot of tea and cooled it in the refrigerator. The refrigerator needed defrosting, but that was more of a job than I had the will to handle just then.

Instead I put on my shoes and walked over to the store and bought some groceries. When I got home I picked up by book and began to think about what I would cook for supper. Despite 17 years of schooling and two degrees that attested to my skills in reading and writing, two weeks of housework were making it nearly impossible for me to read. Keeping the house was making me shut off my mind. I could feel it. I could even begin to explain it. But there was nothing I felt able to do about it. Ideas were a threat to the passivity which I cultivated as a buffer between me and critical self-examination. The activities of housekeeping took just enough awareness to concentrate on the task at hand, but that was enough to allow me to avoid thinking about why I was doing what I was doing. It was hard for me to read anything that required concentration, that demanded a receptive and active mentality. But reading light entertainment made me feel the aimlessness of what I was doing much more acutely. I was forcing myself to give up my powers of concentration out of self-interest (or cowardice, or both), but that meant I was also beginning to diminish the possibility of escape. I was heading toward a situation where I would effectively be a prisoner. But of course my prison was of my own devising. There was nothing except my own problems to keep me from escaping this drudgery and renewing contact with a productive, self-validating task. There was no expectation on anybody's part that I should clean the house. And no recriminations if I didn't clean. Nobody would hassle me if I just walked away from it. Nobody would consider my escape from the house as a desertion, nor would anybody see my desire to keep my mind intact as a threat to his supremacy. All I had to do was get my own shit together.

Then I remembered that I had still not washed the lunch dishes or decided what to make for supper. I washed the dishes and turned over the record and began to prepare a supper of vegetables and rice and a salad. Everybody came home and I kissed my wife and I knew that everybody in the house would want to go to sleep before I did. And that when I went to sleep my body would be tired but my mind would not be. And so I would not really rest. And my tensions would grow.

Everybody said supper was very good.

Afterward, still sitting around the table, I talked about how I wanted to write a story about the demoralizing and destructive effects housekeeping had on me, about what I felt like being a househusband. About how everyday I felt I was losing a little bit more of the resources I need to feel capable and worthwhile. And about how, even so, escape was so far easier for me than for a woman whose education had been designed to teach her to disregard her own instincts and experience and to believe that as a housewife she would be performing her natural task. And that was when Alan, who lives in the goddamn house with me when he's not out there doing all those important things in the world that most men do, said with surprise: ''You mean you've been cleaning up the house every day?''

Jane Lazarre
WHAT FEMINISTS AND FREUDIANS
CAN LEARN FROM EACH OTHER

I began psychoanalysis when I was 18 years old. That was 13 years ago. I was not seduced into this demanding, often painful, inner search by intellectual curiosity, nor by popular fashion, nor even by a desire for an adventurous sex life perfectly packaged within self-fulfilling intimacy. No. It seemed much simpler to me at the time. I was very unhappy. I could find no way out. A friend suggested I try therapy—and the idea of someone dedicated to nothing but listening to me seemed wonderful enough to engage my interest immediately. Even if I had to pay for it, even if only for three hours a week. I had a lot to say and there were nightmares I was desperate to share. It took six years to say and dream it all.

During those six years I was throughly devoted to this inner search of mine. Of course my life outside continued; I attended college, graduated, left home, married, divorced, lived out the detailed demands of my late teens and early 20s. But to my primary passion, I would have sacrificed almost anything. The hidden secrets I carried within me, the amorphous fears, the guilt, these were my real companions. They framed a puzzle I was obsessed with solving; they constituted a world which was far more fascinating to me than the one I had wearily coped with less and less well each day.

In short, I had made what is known as a strong, positive transference. But I didn't know that then. I knew only that this thoroughly new, slowly evolving self-knowledge was not only making me feel better. It was changing my life.

Similarly, it was only toward the end of my search that I realized I had been on the path toward freedom. It was an odd sort of freedom, I found out later, because although it included new options, it also had to do with a self-acceptance I had long counted for lost. But in the first weeks after I terminated analysis, I thought the only boundaries to my perfect liberation were the limitations of my own soul.

So it was with great confidence and pride that I went to my first "Women's Liberation Meeting" in New Haven, Connecticut, in the fall of 1968. There was no "women's movement" yet, though there would be within mere months; there were only 10 or 12 women meeting each Sunday night to talk about freedom, a subject which had become dear to my heart. The transition from the last stage of my analysis was smooth. My analyst, though a man, had been an ardent feminist. And having spent a great deal of time in the past few years learning to forgive my mother for dying, I was passionately ready to embrace womankind. I sat wide-eyed as I found more and more slave-like assumptions in my heart. I listened to the other women recount personal histories with families, and especially with men, which sounded like my own. But there was one area in which I always stood alone, or, as the group grew to 40, 50, and then over 100 woman, with a small minority of others.

Among most of the women there was a deep mistrust of psychotherapy of any sort. Many women had encountered those horrible experiences with analysts which have become so well known by now. Others had read Freud on femininity and were justifiably outraged. Many felt that the inner search, that wonderful journey which had saved my life and turned me into a life-long feminist, was itself fruitless, diversionary, or downright counter-revolutionary.

I was angry and confused; there was a great deal of abuse in the field about which I had been ignorant. Yet there was a validity to my experience which I would not relinquish and which I eventually stopped trying to explain.

Six years later, the feminist critique of Freudian psychoanalysis has become familiar to us all. And though I, as much as anyone, have learned in startled fury of the abuses permeating the profession, I still believe that there are, in psychoanalysis, an essence and, more important, a method which are intrinsically friendly to feminism and which we, as feminists, cannot afford to ignore.

Though I meet many women who have been as greatly

helped by this therapy as any other, few feminists will defend it. If Freud's theory of mind represents a value system which is the child of patriarchy, then women are rightly warned to be wary of the unstated but deftly communicated expectations emanating from the analytic chair behind the couch. Our analysts hold great power over us. So if their sense of the nature of "health" diverges greatly from our own, the dangers for us are extreme. But this is true of any therapy, of any experience in which, by asking for help, we become vulnerable.

Recently a friend of mine was deeply hurt by her therapist. He billed himself as a "radical therapist" of the guru variety. Adoring apostles gathered around him, lived with him, heard him pontificate upon the connections between their neurotic pain and bourgeois values. By the time my friend's complicated emotional problems had all been dumped in the garbage can labeled "bourgeois attitudes toward work," she rebelled. And the therapist exploded in a pretty scary exhibition of patriarchal, narcissistic rage. You don't want to listen to me! he railed. You are fighting the truth. You refuse to join hands with the revolutions! he screamed at her as she ran out of the office.

There is no guarantee that this sort of thing won't happen with any therapist—Freudian, guru or other. But I am convinced that the psychoanalytic theory of technique minimizes such dangers.

First of all, Freud insisted that no one could understand the unconscious of another without coming face to face with her own. A complete personal analysis is the major requirement for psychoanalysts in training. This is a prerequisite to certification by any training institute which derives its theoretical position from Freud, no matter how it may diverge from strict Freudian interpretations in other respects. In fact, the trainee must not only complete a personal analysis, but also a training analysis in which she examines the unconscious reverberations of her reactions to her patients—or her "countertransference." The Freudian analyst, in other words, expresses her commitment to the world of the emotions by traveling deeply and over long periods of time among her own.

That path is charted by Freud in his papers on technique in which he describes concrete methods for reaching our most honest, unadorned selves. This technique cannot be called "psychology" in the academic or clinical sense. It is a western form of the universal search for self-knowledge. Being western, its language is rational and heavily infused with mechanical and biological images, but the central assumption of the technique is the existence of powerful unconscious forces which must be brought into consciousness before any true liberation can begin. Since the unconscious by its very nature is filled with ambivalence and emotional oppositions, which wield great power over our actions, any political movement which fails to take it into account runs the risk of eventually becoming what it sought to replace. In other words, without changing the individual woman, there is no hope of changing her place in history. In order to change ourselves, we must first discover who, below the often-misleading surface, we are.

Who a woman is has usually been defined by who she loves. By the time I was 22, three young men had won my love, calling forth what I was fast discovering to be a pretty self-destructive capacity for devotion. Each boy was a writer. I married the poet and determined to understand and guide him through the torturous demands of his work, giving him, as a gift of love, my own passion for poetry, vowing to be his life-long muse. Now there, if I ever heard one, is a typical story of female oppression at the hands of internalized patriarchal values. I did not consciously hide my own desire to write. I was always writing. But his writing was important, mine a diversion—a familiar example of why women could never be "great" writers. All I ever did was write volume after volume of diaries about my feelings. I agreed with this popular division of literature into sexual polarities. I felt—*I thought I knew*—that the path toward my fulfillment was in loving a man who was an artist.

If I had tried to change this long-nourished pattern on the strength of political liberation or consciousness-raising alone, I think I would never have had the emotional strength to become a writer. I would have been struggling against the deepest layers of myself—a struggle which is always as enervating as it is doomed. The kind of man I always ended up loving was only the tip of the iceberg. On the way down to the base I encountered a *way* of loving which permeated my whole life, which was expressed by most of the primary characters in my life most of the time until it had become my way too, and which was rotten to the core. Understandable—perhaps; forgivable at times—but rotten.

By the time my youthful first marriage had reached its end, I was ready to listen in a new way when my analyst said: And now we must discover what you really want from a man, and what you really want for yourself.

In pursuing those formidable goals, I would have to rely on the three forces which Freud discovered were the mediators, along with dreams, between the conscious and unconscious life. The first of these, and the basic concept in the Freudian theory of technique, is transference.

As months passed by, I had created a relationship with my analyst. He often revealed himself, but the focus was always me. Soon I began to examine that relationship for similarities to every other one in my life, and the parallels were too stark to be ignored. I began to notice my own power in the process of my life. I saw patterns in what was once a hodgepodge of unconnected acts. True, I had no control over the input of other people into the complexity of my experience, but I could take control of my own actions—a possibility which I had not even begun to make use of.

At the same time, I began to talk about things which I could not admit outside the privacy of that room, which had become for me a place of order and comprehension. Emotional tangles came apart as if by magic, because my analyst had become, in a way, a reflection of my strongest self. Secrets emerged. I learned small, personal ways of facing uncomfortable truths. It became safe—with the guidance and the protection of someone who was not involved in my outside life—to remember painful things. All this was part of my transference.

Soon I began to recognize another pattern—the ways I had learned to hide things from myself, or my "resistance." I became acquainted with the walls I had erected against the threat of my real feelings. Mercilessly, I was introduced to my most trustworthy rationalizations. I was involved in a sort of self-criticism which went beyond the sentimental feeling of guilt into the brutally transforming experience of shame. But there was a prize hidden in the battle. I was slowly learning a method of understanding, controlling, and accepting myself, which became the basis for widening my boundaries of choice in all aspects of life. It was not a guarantee. It was only a method.

At a crucial point in my analysis I had what is known as a "transference dream," which collapsed an old and trusted resistance.

I was sitting in a small, dusty bookstore. I was carrying a book by Simone De Beauvoir under my arm. The bookstore owner insisted that it was his copy and that I must pay for it. I repeated that it was mine. So he tied me to a chair and set fire to the bookstore.

Well, it was simple enough to establish that De Beauvoir was a symbol of liberation to me. But who was the bookstore owner? my analyst asked. I began to describe a sordid, sneaky, frightening, little man, summing up finally with a comparison to Peter Lorre. Then, suddenly remembering another dream he had analyzed, in which Edward Albee had appeared and who, it turned out, my analyst knew, I exploded:

"Now don't start telling me Peter Lorre is a great friend of yours and he's a very nice guy."

Why do you say that and why are you so angry? was the obvious question.

Why, indeed? Because my analyst was the bookstore owner who made me feel, three times a week, that I was tied to a chair (couch) and left to roast in a burning house (of my defenses) and who, moreover, was taking credit for my fight for freedom by making me, on top of all other insults, pay for it!

Perhaps it is simplistically tempting to say at this point, filled with liberated glee, Ah yes! Her dream tells the truth, exposing the sexist role of her analyst.

But if I forego that ideological interpretation and look at my anger more closely, I might find even greater nourishment for my feminism, producing real political change in my relationships. Because when my negative feelings for my analyst exploded that evening, the "good patient" syndrome I was locked into exploded along with it. And from the good patient syndrome it was only a short step to the good-little-girl syndrome. For weeks after, I explored the anger and resentment against critical people in my life which I had kept well hidden for years under masks of obedience and passivity. No one had ever told me that I could not be a writer because I was a woman. What I had learned, however, what had been successfully driven into my soul through cultural norm and family habit, was that as a woman I had to please men. As a woman, then, the desire to write was translated into a desire to love male writers. And there were other translations.

The point is that in tearing apart assumptions which were buried in my personal experience, I necessarily questioned many cultural assumptions as well. And as a result of my analysis, I feel a sense of increased assertiveness and a knowledge of self to which I try to give a greater loyalty than the pursuit of any relationship.

Still, the feminist criticism of Freudian theory has been necessary, for ideas which have become so popularized infiltrate our view of ourselves. I, too, rebel at the idea that my biology is my destiny, and my anger grows into full-fledged rage when I realize that, over the centuries of power this myth has enjoyed, I have come to see myself with the oppressor's eye. Recently, I visited some of the major training institutes for analysts in New York to see what impact the women's movement has had on the psychoanalytic establishment. I was determined to pin the analysts down to positions on the classic feminist questions: penis envy, passivity and masochism, social versus psychic causality, and the mother-child relationship.

I wasn't looking for a fight. I suspected that the image of the irredeemably sexist analyst who has not read a line about women since Freud was a pretty simplistic sterotype. In fact, a feminist current has been present in psychoanalytic theory almost from the beginning. Sometimes it is overwhelmed by

---

culture-bound, sexist Victorianism, but it is visible for anyone who cares to read the literature.

For example, in an interview which appeared in *The New York Times Magazine* of February 13, 1972, Anne Roiphe quotes Helena Deutsch, an analyst whom many regard as a classic sell-out to male conditioning:

"Of course, [a woman can work]. There are sociological problems. The society has to help take care of the babies. Russia needs women and has built excellent nurseries.

"I would hope that every girl I would see as a patient would develop a particular passionate interest—something that she could complete and fulfill herself in doing. In addition, I hope she would develop the capacity to feel toward one person a steady, relatively unambivalent love feeling. *This is not really possible in a woman who doesn't have—in her own right— her own area of accomplishment* [my emphasis].

Though one may wish that this passionate, creative woman had contributed more to a non-sexist vision of female sexuality, these are hardly the words of an enemy agent hiding in our ranks.

And the first generation of women analysts were followed by more conscious feminists—Karen Horney, Clara Thompson, Erich Fromm. So that the questioning of such assumptions as penis envy, natural feminine masochism, and passivity had begun long before current feminist psychologists began to unmask the patriarchal lies. Granted there is much theoretical work to do. But the seeds were there from the beginning.

In the 1974 issue of the *Journal of the American Psychoanalytic Association,* which represents the most conservative psychoanalytic institute in the country, the first article is "Problems in Freud's Psychology of Women" by Roy Schafer, in which he not only accepts the feminist criticism of the concepts of penis envy, inferior superego development, and masochism in women, but he also identifies the clinical technique of psychoanalysis as a tool with which the masculine bias in our cultural values can be exposed, allowing us once and for all to understand its dangers.

None of the analysts I spoke to over a three-week period

accepted the notion of penis envy as either inevitable or universal. Feminism has, over the years, effectively undermined the idea of envying a penis just for its magnificent self. Whatever sexism these analysts evidenced as men and products of their time was not bolstered by any simple notion of female biological inferiority. In fact, they find that very few women patients experience such purely anatomical envy.

I have never met a woman who expressed phallic envy on the Freudian model. What I do see everywhere, expressed in social gatherings and political movements, acted out in love affairs, and dramatized for me whenever men suddenly enter a group which was previously all women, what is confessed over and over in women's groups or just among friends, what is depressingly everywhere for us to witness, attesting to the bastion-like strength of traditional social roles, is female passivity in the presence of men, and its more virulent unconscious cousin, masochism.

I remember my shock three years ago when, for the first time, some fathers came to a meeting of our newly created day care center; until that night the center had been almost the sole province of women. We had built it. We ran it. I had been exhilarated by the strength, commitment, and intelligence of these women, who were, with their own hands, renovating a brownstone basement, building equipment, figuring out the administrative problems, all with toddlers and small children clutching at any available arm or leg. And now that we had decided to elect a board of directors, the fathers appeared. The transformation in many of the women was complete. Assertion was muffled by tentative statements ending always in a question mark. Some of the most straightforward speakers said nothing at all. The men were allowed to criticize and judge our efforts with the full support of most of the women. And although some of these men later assumed real responsibilities in the day care center, at that point they were mere visitors at the site of a finished product. Yet they took over. Those of us who objected vehemently were regarded as aggressive liberationists by the women as well as the men.

This association of femininity with passivity pervades every aspect of our social world. It is not that we are told that in order to be feminine we must be passive. Rather, it is assumed that we will relinquish control whenever it is so desired by a man. That is the traditional view of the healthy woman which is reflected in Freud's theory of femininity.

When Freud or anyone else associates passivity, let alone masochism, with psychic health, I know I am in the presence of enemies. Because just as surely as traditional masculinity has bestowed upon us the extremes of war, murder, rape, and a sometimes lethal injury to the ability to love, traditional femininity, wrapped in the seductive ribbons of self-denial and reeking of the smell of impotence, will kill off the delicate flame of any spirit.

None of the analysts I spoke with were rigid or even defensive about their position on this question. At least consciously, they acknowledged that Freud's theory of femininity was outdated and sexist.

So the impact of feminism upon some once-precious psychoanalytic notions has been very real. I wondered if the political awareness of the last few years had also affected the frequently narrow psychoanalytic view of the causes of neurosis.

Three years ago, I was a student for a time at the Institute for Practicing Psychotherapists. My most frequent argument with the analysts who were my teachers concerned their dismissal of social and political causality, the way they had of moving the entire universe inside the insanely cramped quarters of the individual mind.

In one class, the analyst described a black male patient who complained of his feelings of being pursued, disliked, threatened. It seems painfully obvious that such feelings are not merely the sign of some purely personal paranoid fantasy. But that's precisely how the man's fears were interpreted, no matter that a few of us protested that the "fantasy" on some level was true. The analyst and most of the class repeatedly and contentedly banished the messy, outside world from the room which, for me, had become worse than the most sterile laboratory.

A bias toward intra-psychic causality of problems still pervades the field. After all, therapy is an investigation of the personal, private experience of one person, of the details which make each of our experiences different. But both analyst and student are giving more credence to social and political influences now than my teacher did three years ago. There has been a great deal of cultural criticism in the last few years, much dramatic exposure of the limitations and injustices in our society. What this means in analytic terms is that the concept of health is being broadened to include some unconventional behavior which would previously have been defined as sick (for example, the recent official change in attitude toward homosexuality). Since few would point to the traditional, well-adjusted American as a paragon of psychic health, the implication for those who rebel is obvious.

But if analysts are bold and critical about penis envy and female masochism, unambivalent about the need for greater assertiveness in women, and more likely to see that pathology may reside as much in social norms as in the individual who conflicts with them, they become tentative and hesitant, almost ignorant, when the discussion turns to the connections between the oppression of women and the kind of expectations conferred upon her as a mother.

This is the crunch for feminists, too. We have made enormous progress in the last few years changing our image of ourselves. Most of the childless women I know are living lives they could not have lived five years ago. Their priorities have changed. Their relationships with men and women have dramatically changed. Their clothes have changed. Even their needs have changed. But the women's movement has given scant attention to the experience of motherhood. That experience has been sloughed off in a crush of negative descriptions of the difficulties of motherhood which, although funny at times and even relieving, do not begin to approach an understanding of the enormity of this part of our lives.

Several of the analysts I visited told me about an English psychologist named Winecott, who has come up with a theory of "the good enough mother." I gather the idea includes an attempt to demystify the image of the perfect mother whom the psychologists and psychoanalysts, in the company of most of western religion and philosophy, have tied to any hope for psychic health. She crashes her whip daily, this mother-goddess, over the backs of merely human mothers, who are all sentenced to that special, miserable doom of spending a lifetime reaching for what is by its very nature unattainable. Mothers have been burdened by psychologists' assertions that we are the source of all psychic evil in our children. For the individual mother this often translates into a fear that one false move on her part, one impulse which falls short of perfection, one, God forbid, mean or selfish act will blight her child for life.

Now, much too late, and as tentatively as only the obsessively scientific can be, we are being told that a "good enough" mother—i.e., a faulted, imperfect, selfish, impatient, human woman—is not necessarily sacrificing her children's mental health on the altar of her own limitations. Well, that's something like telling blacks that, although we whites have no particular plan for social change, we have decided that, perhaps, they are not inferior; or, like the Pope, a few years back, granting the innocence of the Jews in the killing of Jesus.

No one has come to grips with the real issue, which is women's all too exclusive claim to the child-care burden. Analysts who in their practice certainly must have heard a lot about what real mothers feel are strangely reticent on this point. Perhaps this is partly because any critical re-evaluation of motherhood will have some challenging implications for fathers.

In a recent book called *Women, Culture and Society* (edited by Rosaldo and Lamphere) the authors suggest that, although women are oppressed in all societies, they are least so when men share child-rearing and homemaking responsibilities. This factor, it seems, is much more significant than whether or not women function outside these roles. I believe it. Most men who will support women's rights to equal opportunities outside the home balk and stutter at the notion that *they* march into their homes and become better acquainted with the enormous task of bringing up their children.

I spoke with one analyst who openly admitted his difficulties around the question of fatherhood. His wife, by his description, is a strong woman whom he admires and whose work he respects. But lately, he has been asked to help care for their child and the house. This is a successful man, a respected psychiatrist as well as a psychoanalyst, a person who has touched all the bases and is on his way to a home run in the masculine game of professional achievement. Caring for his child, clearly, means sacrificing some of that. He reminded me of several close male friends of mine who are caught in the same conflict. How much ambition and career success are they willing to jeopardize in the service of becoming responsible, loving fathers? and remaining the husbands of feminist wives?

Anything? I asked. The doctor didn't know. But part of his answer included a recognition, which grows out of his analytic training, that he has to search his own unconscious for his difficulties in changing. He has to find, he said, and give expression to the "feminine" in himself.

That kind of willingness to be self-examining continually impresses me as the strength which emerges from psychoanalysis. And I see a danger, therefore, that in criticizing Freud's theory for its sexism, or in lumping all analysts with the individual sexists we may have met, we will begin to associate feminist psychology with mechanical behaviorism or conditioning therapy. This is the philosophical basis of many of the popular new group therapies which represent a masculine bias at its worst in their emphasis on continual confrontation, on action and performance, and on quick and easy solutions. Freud's technique, in its recognition of the unconscious and its respect for the slow process of change, depends on the use and development of precisely those qualities which, down through the ages, have been called "feminine." The analyst and the patient are trained in the use of insight, intuition, non-verbal communication. Knowledge emerges from personal experience, the inner world is given the greatest importance in defining the self, and the analyst's ability to identify sympathetically with the patient is the first step in helping her.

Several analysts have told me of their preference for women patients, the reason being, they say, that women already know so much about self-examination. (That's what we have always done.) Free association is easily learned. And, most important, a woman's sense of identity is more likely to come from who she is rather than from what she does.

Such qualities are not usually highly developed among men. They are the antithesis of the masculine mystique. They have been repressed in men and reserved in women in the service of patriarchy and capitalism.

I have always felt that the best of feminism includes an appreciation for what has been denigrated as "feminine." So I am not surprised that there are many feminist psychoanalysts and therapists today. I would like to believe that, like me, they found in psychoanalysis and feminism two sources for personal liberation which have nourished each other and which point toward a more humanistic radicalism than we have known in the past.

It was with this hope that I attended the Women and Psychology Conference held this fall by the Women's Psychotherapy Referral Service.

Sitting in the auditorium, I sense shared assumptions here. We know where much traditional psychology has failed us. We understand in our gut how some "experts" have become so onanistically involved with their own definitions and projections about women that they have left us, the real, complex, many-faceted women, standing on the side, excluded in a puff of pipe smoke.

But these are also women who have personally confronted the unconscious—with all its natural ambivalence, childish, gaping needs as well as strengths, ugliness as well as beauty, pain as well as anger.

I am at this conference looking for connections between personal and cultural change. I am hoping to hear voices which are political, but not at the price of personal honesty.

A young analyst speaks directly to this point.

"I am a feminist therapist," she says, "but I cannot simply agree with radical statements made by my patients. As a therapist, my job is to understand how a person arrived at those statements—in other words I must investigate the 'not me'" (a Sullivanian concept based on the unconscious). She is saying that the role of the therapist is not ideological. Yes; she is right.

But then, she looks worried. Perhaps she senses that she is about to go over the mark. She asks us, "Why should I change society, if I can manipulate it? If I change, does it matter if others do?"

The audience groans and I am with them. She has fallen into the pit; the world inside the mind has become all.

"Now you may think this is a middle-of-the-road position," she continues, trying to compromise.

"NO! REACTIONARY!" yell some of the younger women. They see that she is preaching psychic alienation. And just as surely as the denial of ambivalence is the constant, inherent danger of the political life, the denial of social responsibility is the most crippling possibility of a personal search which is cut off from its culture and thus whisked impotently out of history.

Dr. Helen Brody offers case presentations in her workshop in order to illustrate the role of political values in therapy, describing how she and a traditional therapist might interpret a case differently. Ultimately, there is no solution to the disproportionate power this confers upon the therapist. You must share the most important values with your therapist or you are in trouble.

In this room, the overriding value is freedom. Dr. Brody describes a woman whose life revolves around new clothes, a choice between a husband and lover, and her own beauty. She must always be the passive recipient of admiration. Although her limitations are severe, Dr. Brody explains, a traditional therapist might not even notice. A man in the same situation, however, would instantly be classified as sick. Dr. Brody had presented the case in a class for therapists. A male psychiatrist had said, harshly, "She is a manipulative woman." Yes, Dr. Brody confirms more softly, she is a manipulative woman; she is desperate for love. She doesn't have many choices.

This is a conference, not a lecture, and so I am here partly to examine my own choices. But, like so many feminist conferences, this one doesn't treat motherhood as an important issue, as an experience which deserves examination in itself. Motherhood is viewed as political only when modified by a livelier subject, like lesbian motherhood or the single mother. Selma Guber runs a workshop on the single parent, and since she is the only one who mentions motherhood at all, it is to her workshop that I go.

There are three married women besides me in a room full of single mothers. The four of us agree that we are there (1) because motherhood is central to our lives and (2) because we suspect that because we work, we have many things in common with other working mothers, single or married. We all live with the anger-guilt-love cycle in relation to our children. But, although several women insist that we stop and explore these emotions, there is great resistance in the room. I see again that it is easier to face change as working women or as sexual beings than it is as mothers. In our motherhood, we still live in the same prison of mythology as we always have. We have merely exposed the negative aspects of motherhood; as feminists, we have not yet begun to talk about the love. I suspect that feminists are as frightened as anyone else by the incredible quality of intimacy involved in parenthood.

The capacity to love is the strength women have developed and sometimes perfected through the ages, the gift we have grabbed out of the history of our oppression. But we are frightened by the distorted directions in which this power has sometimes led us. In its service we have been forced to neglect, even repress, our capacity for creative independence. So that in our polarized world, men and women alike stand as thwarted human beings.

But the struggle for unity has begun. The central problem for feminist therapists is the search for an androgynous understanding of personality. For in order to avoid the most ironic of defeats, in which we join the men in their form of half-life— autonomy at the expense of intimacy—we must be careful not to lose what we have.

That danger is very real because, to a greater or lesser degree, all of our characters—men and women—have been built upon the masculine value system. Whenever I meet someone who seems influenced to a lesser degree by these values, I feel a sense of peaceful, uncompetitive relief. I guess that's the feeling men have always looked for in the traditional wife.

One morning, instead of the fashionable offices I had been frequenting, I walked up several flights to a small Village apartment. There I met Connie Brown, a therapist and a feminist who has been nurtured on the politics of left-wing America. She attends the Women's Guild for Psychoanalysis, a small training institute which was started by a woman who wanted to train ordinary women to do therapy. The institute is based on the three-part guild structure of apprentice, journeywoman, and master. Connie Brown is about to become a journeywoman. And although we spoke of many contradictions in our lives which seemed to defy solution, there was no irresolvable conflict for her between psychoanalysis and the best of feminism. There had been once, when, in an early consciousness-raising group she had been severely criticized for being in analysis herself. Now, years later, she has moved away from the polarization of the personal and the political and seems to have found a way of integrating them without retreating to a vegetable garden in Vermont.

I think this integration is partly due to her training. There are no academic requirements in the guild, but the same three-pronged training found in the more traditional institutes prevails: theoretical study, personal analysis, and training analysis.

This guild must be the creation of an extraordinary woman, I remark.

But, no, I am told, she doesn't seem to be so—though possibly she is. One has, rather, the sense of an ordinary person.

I am stunned by this remark, offered so quietly by the young woman sitting at a kitchen table while she makes me coffee. For this recognition of your own *ordinary* humanity is a part of every creative analysis.

"I will not be mediocre! I am special!" is the cry of the neurotic. Yet I know that when I am most able to accept myself for being *only* human, I am best at loving others; it is in our ordinary humanness that we are linked. And only within the context of that recognition can my specialness emerge. As only within that context can I, without domination, respect yours.

As parents, too, we cannot avoid this truth; the more we see our children as being everlastingly special, magnificently different from all other children, the more we suffocate their real individuality by the heavy weight of our unreachable expectations. Fortunately, they want always and infuriatingly to be ordinary, to do what their friends do. The favorite child, expected to stand out, suffers as much as the rejected one.

As Connie Brown talks about her work, I begin to see that she uses the concepts of transference and resistance in the service of reinforcing this relatedness to others. They are of supreme importance in her practice as she tries to facilitate the inner search. She finds that, often, she says very little, because her patient has so much to say; once begun, the process is self-perpetuating. And over and over again, she is impressed with the importance of the unconscious in the creation of relationships.

There is a caring for others that is born out of a caring for oneself. This is the ratification in clinical experience of a truth which feminists have always known. Connie marvels as her patients begin to see themselves as merely human and, paradoxically, thus learn to nurture themselves, to grow, to respect their own integrity. They are not to be interfered with, she asserts. But she says all of this softly, almost tentatively, belying the strength of her words.

We tried to do this for each other in the women's movement. When a consciousness-raising group was good, it was good because we saw ourselves in each other, found that we were not that different after all. In those days, we talked a lot about the value of "feminine" qualities as we learned to love ourselves and other women. We shrank from hierarchal organization, denying the need for leaders. We took care of each other's children and searched for a lost respect for our mothers. More than anything, we tried to become conscious of where our strength as women lay. And while we demanded our right to the hitherto masculine privilege of commitment to independent work, throwing off one by one the silly trappings of socially defined femininity, we were determined to cling to our heritage. For we had lived all of our lives with men who were certainly as crippled in their way as we were in ours. Perhaps more so. And we did not seek to emulate them.

Those of us who continued to love our men had no alternative but to help them change along with ourselves. While we struggled in learning to be autonomous, we tried to teach them the secrets of intimacy, and we taught by demanding that they give us a kind of love which our mothers and grandmothers had insisted men could never give.

Some men have had the courage to touch "the feminine" in themselves as they broke down a few of the bastions of their masculinity, like rugged individualism, obsessive competition, physical affection which verges on violence, ambition which runs all the way up the continuum to genocide. They are finding that such guarantees of virility are more dispensable than they thought—and without the guarantees, a more fulfilling manhood becomes possible.

None of this comes easy. Feminist consciousness does not come easy. Sacrifices litter the path. But political ideals are easily betrayed by the powerful ambivalence of unconscious desires.

I may want with all my heart to love gentle, emotional, considerate men. It will matter little if, unconsciously, I am still drawn to men who, in their own unconscious devotion to the harshest demands of masculinity, continue to objectify and hurt women. The unconscious is the source of sexual attraction. That is why it has always been a mystery.

The romance of that mystery is gone for me. I will gladly sacrifice the painful magic for a nurturing friendship chosen in full awareness that I am refusing satisfaction to some of my deepest and most destructive needs. I can make that choice only if I have learned to claim the ugliness of certain desires as my own—that process of recognition and self-accpetance which for me began in psychoanalysis and which never really ends.

No self-knowledge has ever come easy for me. But when I began, in my analysis, to explore all the intricate layers of my isolation, within the torment of my unanswered needs, I was looking for a way of loving others which would not, for once, destroy me. That is also what I seek as a feminist.

Grace Paley
THE USED-BOY RAISERS

There were two husbands disappointed by eggs.

I don't like them that way either, I said. Make your own eggs. They sighed in unison. One man was livid; one was pallid.

There isn't a drink around here, is there? asked Livid.

Never find one here, said Pallid. Don't look; driest damn house. Pallid pushed the eggs away, pain and disgust his escutcheon.

Livid said, Now really, isn't there a drink? Beer? he hoped.

Nothing, said Pallid, who'd been through the pantries, closets, and refrigerators looking for a white shirt.

You're damn right, I said. I buttoned the high button of my powder-blue duster. I reached under the kitchen table for a brown paper bag full of an embroidery which asked God to Bless Our Home.

I was completing this motto for the protection of my sons, who were also Livid's. It is true that some months earlier, from a far place—the British plains in Africa—he had written hospitably to Pallid; I do think they're fine boys, you understand. I love them too, but Faith is their mother and now Faith is your wife. I'm so much away. If you want to think of them as yours, old man, go ahead.

Why, thank you, Pallid had replied, airmail, overwhelmed. Then he implored the boys, when not in use, to play in their own room. He made all efforts to be kind.

Now as we talked of time past and upon us, I pierced the ranch house that nestles in the shade of a cloud and a Norway maple, just under the golden script.

Ha-ha, said Livid, dripping coffee on his pajama pants, you'll never guess whom I met up with, Faith.

Who? I asked.

Saw your old boy friend Clifford at the Green Coq. He looks well. One thing must be said, he addressed Pallid, she takes good care of her men.

True, said Pallid.

How is he? I asked coolly. What's he doing? I haven't seen him in two years.

Oh, you'll never guess. He's marrying. A darling girl. She was with him. Little tootsies, little round bottom, little tummy—she must be twenty-two, but she looks seventeen. One long yellow braid down her back. A darling girl. Stubby nose, fat little underlip. Her eyes put on in pencil. Shoulders down like a dancer . . . slender neck. Oh, darling, darling.

You certainly observed her, said Pallid.

I have a functioning retina, said Livid. Then he went on. Better watch out, Faith. You'd be surprised, the dear little chicks are hatching out all over the place. All the sunny schoolgirls rolling their big black eyes. I hope you're really settled this time. To me, whatever is under the dam is in another county; however, in my life you remain an important person historically, he said. And that's why I feel justified in warning you. I must warn you. Watch out, sweetheart! he said, leaning forward to whisper harshly and give me a terrible bellyache.

What's all this about? asked Pallid innocently. In the first place, she's settled . . . and then she's still an attractive woman. Look at her.

Oh yes, said Livid, looking. An attractive woman. Magnificent, sometimes.

We were silent for several seconds in honor of that generous remark.

Then Livid said, Yes, magnificent, but I just wanted to warn you, Faith.

He pushed his eggs aside finally and remembered Clifford. A mystery wrapped in an enigma . . . I wonder why he wants to marry.

I don't know, it just ties a man down, I said.

And yet, said Pallid seriously, what would I be without marriage? In luminous recollection—a gay dog, he replied.

At this moment, the boys entered: Richard the horse thief and Tonto the crack shot.

Daddy! they shouted. They touched Livid, tickled him, unbuttoned his pajama top, whistled at the several gray hairs coloring his chest. They tweaked his ear and rubbed his beard the wrong way.

Well, well, he cautioned. How are you boys, have you been well? You look fine. Sturdy. How are your grades? he inquired. He dreamed that they were just up from Eton for the holidays.

I don't go to school, said Tonto. I go to the park.

I'd like to hear the child read, said Livid.

Me. I can read, Daddy, said Richard. I have a book with a hundred pages.

Well, well, said Livid. Get it.

I kindled a fresh pot of coffee. I scrubbed cups and harassed Pallid into opening a sticky jar of damson-plum jam. Very shortly, what could be read, had been, and Livid, knotting the tie strings of his pants vigorously, approached me at the stove. Faith, he admonished, that boy can't read a tinker's damn. Seven years old.

Eight years old, I said.

Yes, said Pallid, who had just remembered the soap cabinet and was rummaging in it for a pint. If they were my sons in actuality as they are in everyday life, I would send them to one of the good parochial schools in the neighborhood where reading is taught. Reading, St. Bartholomew's, St. Bernard's, St. Joseph's.

Livid became deep purple and gasped. Over my dead body. *Merde,* he said in deference to the children. I've said yes, you may think of the boys as your own, but if I ever hear they've come within an inch of that church, I'll run you through, you bastard. I was fourteen years old when in my own good sense I walked out of that grotto of deception, head up. You sonofabitch, I don't give a damn how *au courant* it is these days, how gracious to be seen under a dome on Sunday. . . . Shit! Hypocrisy. Corruption. Cave dwellers. Idiots. Morons.

Recalling childhood and home, poor Livid writhed in his

seat. Pallid listened, head to one side, his brows gathering the onsets of grief.

You know, he said slowly, we iconoclasts . . . we free-thinkers . . . We latter-day masons . . . we idealists . . . we dreamers . . . we are never far from our nervous old mother, the Church. She is never far from us.

Wherever we are, we can hear, no matter how faint, her hourly bells, tolling the countryside, reverberating in the cities, bringing to our civilized minds the passionate deed of Mary. Every hour on the hour we are startled with remembrance of what was done for us. FOR US.

Livid muttered in great pain, Those bastards, oh oh oh, those contemptible, goddamnable bastards. Do we have to do the nineteenth century all over again? All right, he bellowed, facing us all, I'm ready. That Newman! He turned to me for approval.

You know, I said, this subject has never especially interested me. It's your little dish of lava.

Pallid spoke softly, staring past the arched purple windows of his soul. I myself, although I lost God a long time ago, have never lost faith.

What the hell are you talking about, you moron? roared Livid.

I have never lost my love for the wisdom of the Church of the World. When I go to sleep at night, I inadvertently pray. I also do so when I rise. It is not to God, it is to that unifying memory out of childhood. The first words I ever wrote were: What are the sacraments? Faith, can you ever forget your old grandfather intoning Kaddish? It will sound in your ears forever.

Are you kidding? I was furious to be drawn into their conflict. Kaddish? What do I know about Kaddish? Who's dead? You know my opinions perfectly well. I believe in the Diaspora, not only as a fact but a tenet. I'm against Israel on technical grounds. I'm very disappointed that they decided to become a nation in my lifetime. I believe in the Diaspora. After all, they *are* the chosen people. Don't laugh. They really are. But once they're huddled in one little corner of a desert, they're like anyone else: Frenchies, Italians, temporal nation-alities. Jews have one hope only—to remain a remnant in the basement of world affairs—no, I mean something else—a splinter in the toe of civilizations, a victim to aggravate the conscience.

Livid and Pallid were astonished at my outburst, since I rarely express my opinion on any serious matter but only live out my destiny, which is to be, until my expiration date, laughingly the servant of man.

I continued. I hear they don't even look like Jews any more. A bunch of dirt farmers with no time to read.

They're your own people, Pallid accused, dilating in the nostril, clenching his jaw. And they're under the severest attack. This is not the time to revile them.

I had resumed my embroidery. I sighed. My needle was now deep in the clouds which were pearl gray and late afternoon. I am only trying to say that they aren't meant for geographies but for history. They are not supposed to take up space but to continue in time.

They looked at me with such grief that I decided to consider all sides of the matter. I said, Christ probably had all that trouble—now that you mention it—because he knew he was going to gain the whole world but he forgot Jerusalem.

When you married us, said Pallid, and accused me, didn't you forget Jerusalem?

I never forget a thing, I said. Anyway, guess what. I just read somewhere that England is bankrupt. The country is wadded with installment paper.

Livid's hand trembled as he offered Pallid a light. Nonsense, he said. That's not true. Nonsense. The great British Island is the tight little fist of the punching arm of the Commonwealth.

What's true is true, I said, smiling.

Well, I said, since no one stirred, do you think you'll ever get to work today? Either of you?

Oh, my dear, I haven't even seen you and the boys in over a year. It's quite pleasant and cozy here this morning, said Livid.

Yes, isn't it? said Pallid, the surprised host. Besides, it's Saturday.

How do you find the boys? I asked Livid, the progenitor.

American, American, rowdy, uncontrolled. But you look well, Faith. Plumper, but womanly and well.

Very well, said Pallid, pleased.

But the boys, Faith. Shouldn't they be started on something? Just lining up little plastic cowboys. It's silly, really.

They're so young, apologized Pallid, the used-boy raiser.

You'd both better go to work, I suggested, knotting the pearl-gray late-afternoon thread. Please put the dishes in the sink first. Please. I'm sorry about the eggs.

Livid yawned, stretched, peeked at the clock, sighed. Saturday or no, alas, my time is not my own. I've got an appointment downtown in about forty-five minutes, he said.

I do too, said Pallid. I'll join you on the subway.

I'm taking a cab, said Livid.

I'll split it with you, said Pallid.

They left for the bathroom, where they shared things nicely—shaving equipment, washstand, shower, and so forth.

I made the beds and put the aluminum cot away. Livid would find a hotel room by nightfall. I did the dishes and organized the greedy day; dinosaurs in the morning, park in the afternoon, peanut butter in between, and at the end of it all, to reward us for a week of beans endured, a noble rib roast with little onions, dumplings, and pink applesauce.

Faith, I'm going now, Livid called from the hall. I put my shopping list aside and went to collect the boys, who were wandering among the rooms looking for Robin Hood. Go say goodbye to your father, I whispered.

Which one? they asked.

The real father, I said. Richard ran to Livid. They shook hands manfully. Pallid embraced Tonto and was kissed eleven times for his affection.

Goodbye now, Faith, said Livid. Call me if you want anything at all. Anything at all, my dear. Warmly with sweet propriety he kissed my cheek. Ascendant, Pallid kissed me with considerable business behind the ear.

Goodbye, I said to them.

I must admit that they were at last clean and neat, rather

attractive, shiny men in their thirties, with the grand affairs of the day ahead of them. Dark night, the search for pleasure and oblivion were well ahead. Goodbye, I said, have a nice day. Goodbye, they said once more, and set off in pride on paths which are not my concern.

Uta West
IF LOVE IS THE ANSWER,
WHAT IS THE QUESTION?

The myth that falling in love will solve all our emotional problems and provide us with instant fulfillment has not really been weakened by recent cultural upheavals—the sexual revolution, women's liberation, or the terminal illness of the institution of marriage. Nor has outward emancipation noticeably diminished women's emotional slavery. Without seeking legal ties or any other firm commitments, the New Woman more than ever is desperate to fall in love and "have a relationship." A lot of men know this and exploit it, consciously or not—"I dig you, baby, but I must be free" is a sentiment that cannot be disputed by the would-be liberated woman. But she is stuck with her needs, her dreams and hopes, her ravenous hunger for love, sweet love, all you need is love, that's the only thing that there just ain't enough of. The pop songs still peddle the same old wares, the same self-deprecating attitudes, even if the language is hip and up-to-date.

That psychosexual abnormality known as falling in love, with its heady mixture of ecstasy and misery, has always had and no doubt will always have its place in the human psyche. But it is *not* a basis for cohabitation . . . let alone a lifetime contract. Whatever needs and desires it answers for a time, falling in love tends to create problems rather than solve them. The most famous and violent "fallings" occur with partners who are totally unsuitable from society's point of view (Romeo and Juliet, Tristan and Isolde), and/or unsuitable in terms of personal temperament and everyday living. History and legend abound with evidence showing that falling in love can be very dangerous. Anyway, the idea that we have the right not only to hope but to expect that we will fall in love and marry the one we love is a very recent notion. In former times and in other cultures, falling in love was the stuff for jokes, heartache, or tragedy. It seldom impinged on the normal business of family, marriage, and children.

Insecurity is practically built into the situation. A girl in love has made herself helplessly vulnerable—she has delivered herself into the hands of just one person and her center of gravity depends on him; she has forfeited her peace of mind and will be tossed between joy and sorrow at his whim. Wouldn't you say this is a mixed blessing, at best? In fact, it's rather frightening, if you think about it. But you won't. Because this dependency is precisely what you want. Simone de Beauvoir has pointed out that it is agonizing for a woman to assume responsibility for her own life. "Love for a woman is a mystic, a religious experience. She desires to . . . amalgamate her inessential self to some higher being—God or lover . . . the annihilation of love is, in fact, an avid will to exist. When a woman gives herself completely, she hopes her idol will give her at once possession of herself and of the universe he represents."

More recently, Germaine Greer warned: "Women must recognize in the cheap ideology of being in love the essential persuasion to take an irrational, self-destructive step. Such obsession has nothing to do with love, for love is not swoon or mania but a cognitive act, indeed the only way to grasp the innermost core of personality."

One might envy Greer her assurance, did not our knowledge of her personal life suggest that she, too, might have difficulty distinguishing between being in love and loving.

Elizabeth Janeway explains that when a woman tries to lose herself she seems not so much to be giving up her own identity as asking for the lover's, and that is hard to grant. "When the response is felt to be inadequate, unsatisfied greed is added to anxiety; highly unpleasant emotions to encounter where one has been told to look for pleasure. Both can arise where human relationships gather about themselves disproportionate feelings of hope and obligation." According to Janeway, this feeling of connection as obligation haunts our era.

It haunts, in particular, the male of our species. Men, too, dream of falling in love with the "right" woman. But their longing is tempered by a very strong fear of love, despite the fact that they have less at stake. James Stephens described the crucial difference:

"A man in love submits only to a woman, a partial, individual and temporary submission, but a woman surrenders to the very God of love himself, and is not only deprived of her personal liberty but is even infected in her mental processes by this crafty obsession."

One might think women would shun this "crafty obsession" like the plague. But we go on courting emotional disaster with an alacrity that stuns the mind. What is so marvelous about being in love? Why is it worth so much turmoil, anxiety, and grief?

Sophie, who is twenty-two, an artist and a fashion model, was one of those who tried to answer my question. Tall, slender, with delicate features, her looks and manner reflect the soft, fey, diffident style currently in vogue. Sophie left home at the age of sixteen—she comes from a well-to-do Connecticut family torn by alcoholism and divorce—and has traveled around the country, visiting communes. She has several love affairs behind her.

"I used to believe I would find the key in another person," says Sophie. "Because I once had this psychedelic experience without drugs—with a man. But, of course, after I opened up with this man, six months later everything closed up again, to the point where I couldn't even feel anybody touching me. I had to suffer, I had to be a martyr and rise above it. And I picked the worst bastard in the world—well, maybe he really wasn't such a bastard, but I was willing to be such a martyr that I stayed on no matter what he did.

"I was creating the whole thing for myself," she continued. "It was such absolute crap; it was my first love affair and it had to be a certain way. And I really didn't love him at all."

Sophie thinks she knows better now. "You're your own key, and you have to learn to open yourself to yourself." Does that mean she's given up on love? Not a chance. For the past year she's been living with a young man, eighteen years old, and here's what she has to say about that:

"When you're in love, you love yourself, and that's what makes everything beautiful. When I was first with Tommy, I never looked in mirrors. And when I did, I looked beautiful, whereas most of the time I look grotesque to myself."

By all objective standards, Sophie is lovely. I asked what happened when the vibrations of daily life cracked the mirror, or shattered it altogether. She grew thoughtful. "You have to outlast the bad humps," she said, "and slowly work yourself back to the same point, on a more realistic level."

I suggested that love affairs might have a built-in time limit; that you were fortunate if you could develop in parallel ways. "You have to fight for that," said Sophie, with a look of determination that indicated she would stubbornly hang in there, way past the deadline . . . would play the martyr again, if necessary, in order to "work it out."

The belief that you are supposed to "work" on love, that you have to "fight" for it, seems to be a powerful one indeed. The woman feels it's up to her to make the relationship succeed, and will accept endless suffering and humiliation in the belief that it's the price one has to pay for love. She is convinced that being in love is essential to her self-esteem and that she is incomplete without it. And so she will put up with all kinds of abuse, ignore all the signs of deterioration, all the damage to her psyche (and her partner's) in order to keep the dream of love alive.

"It's the imagination that's involved," said a woman who has had an affair with a married man for fourteen years. "I'm a tremendous builder. And I have erected a mighty structure. And that, if you'll forgive me, is what love is about."

It is interesting to note that such an attitude implies, along with much self-control and self-denial, no small degree of arrogance. *She* is the builder, the one who controls the well-being of the relationship. But think of the responsibility . . . think of the *guilt* when that mighty structure becomes dismantled, as it so often does, despite our best efforts!

"It must be an incredible accident," said a man, recently

divorced, "when people stay in sync over long periods of time. When they get over bad parts and stagger along, and grow, or even dwindle, but in sync. The point is, when you get out of sync, there's nothing left—not even fights. Who are you, and what are you doing in my bed?"

The woman would reply that you have to "work" at staying in sync, though what exactly this work consists of is not very clear. It would seem to be largely a matter of compliance, devotion, and certain romantic trappings, which evidently symbolize far more to the woman than they do to the man.

Heather is an exponent of the work ethic in love. She is thirty-two, lives in London with her seven-year-old daughter, and works hard at a career in publishing. She also works hard at her relationships with men. A big, beautiful woman with melting dark eyes, Heather gives the impression of being at once very capable and very feminine. Born in Ceylon, raised in provincial England, she married young, against the advice of family and friends. Though the marriage was, in her words, a "disaster" almost from the start, she stuck it out for five years—the last two spent mostly "waiting," alone with her infant daughter. She then lived with another man for five years, and this affair has recently come to an end.

During those ten years, Heather was out of work less than a year, in order to have her baby, and often during her marriage she was the sole provider. "When we were both still at university," she explains, "I would work at the post office during Christmas vacations, sorting mail and so on, but no, *he* couldn't, because he had to do a lot of reading, which usually meant drinking in the pubs." However, Heather admits to being completely dependent emotionally on her men. "I think I am too much of a romantic and regard that as part of my weakness," she says. "To me, a relationship is something that has to be very closely looked after . . . guarded. Everything has to be right; literally, candles on the dinner table every night. I'd go to great lengths to prepare things nicely so that when Raymond [her recent lover] got back from work, which was always late, around nine, we would sit and eat together.

Occasionally, it was a bit difficult when he would insist on taking his meal and going to sit in front of the telly."

I remarked that a man might just not feel like having dinner by candlelight *every* night. And in fact, he left her for a girl who was flighty and irresponsible. "I think he was a little overpowered by what I felt for him," Heather says ruefully. "He thought he did not love me as much as I loved him." She admits that when there is a man in her life, he comes first, taking precedence to a large extent over her own child. Obviously, not all men find the burden of such devotion to their liking.

Having overinvested in romance, modern woman has become a beggar. She grovels for a crumb of love. No longer does she need a man so she may have food in her belly and a roof over her head, to protect her or secure her social position. When she *had* those needs and suffered in a bad marriage, at least she did not offer up her soul for a few soft words or an orgasm. She had her pride, the dignity of someone dealing with and making the best of a harsh reality.

But what are we to make of the sophisticated urban woman, winner of the sexual revolution, conqueror of the feminine mystique, the triumphant product of centuries of psychic labor. What is the meaning of that look of hunger and desperation in her eyes? Why does she fidget so nervously with her false eyelashes? She has another date with the assistant buyer in her office, who earns $3,000 a year less than she does, and maybe tonight he'll be able to get it up. She knows she must be patient and relaxed, but she is anxious and the martinis haven't taken the edge off the jitters. Her analyst has explained it all—it's *his* problem, nothing to do with her, but why, oh why, does it happen so often? What is it she does wrong, or fails to do right? She checks the mirror, but it tells her nothing. She knows she looks good, as good as she can look and better than most. She knows how to make a man comfortable, how to talk when called for and be quiet at other times, how to let him know she likes sex without being aggressive. Her apartment is charming—her books, her records, her cuisine . . . everything is beyond reproach. She appears intact, but the pain of lovelessness has hollowed her out; loneliness has emptied her till there is nothing but this enormous, aching void inside, growing bigger every day, pushing against the glossy outer shell. She reads the latest books on sex; of course she is "good in bed." But she does not really enjoy sex . . . she cannot enjoy sex while she is consumed with anxiety and sorrow about the coldness and inhumanity of her sexual encounters.

Rachel is one such victim of the liberation void. Outwardly, she is the quintessential New York career girl—chic, energetic, efficient. Arriving from Oklahoma five years ago, she has "made it," at the age of twenty-eight, in the toughest business in the toughest city in the world. With her long-legged, long-haired Junior Miss looks, she is at once ingénue and elegant. All her childhood dreams have come true, she told me. She wanted to be a fashion buyer on Fifth Avenue and she is. She wanted to go to Europe, and she goes at least twice a year. A glamorous life, yet Rachel spends a lot of evenings alone, wearing the same old jeans and sweater, watching TV—depressed, confused, wondering what's missing. Or else she's running around, to her analyst, her gym class, her consciousness-raising—getting tired, wondering what's *still* missing. It is, of course, the Dream of Dreams: Love and Marriage.

At the time of our talk she was "living" with a young man who did not suit her at all; she admitted she had not considered Carl a marital possibility "even for thirty seconds." Nevertheless, she asked him to move in with her the first night they got together. "At the time I met Carl I had a tremendous need for somebody . . . *anybody* . . . around me. I'd gone out with a lot of men and not found anybody I was attracted to, for a very long time. Then one freak night some guy comes over and I was just so *ready* for it . . . someone I could dig, mentally and physically. . . ."

I asked why she had to have him *living* with her. We were then neighbors and I knew her well enough to point out that

---

Carl spent more nights *away* from her apartment than in it; that she'd wait for him to call and let her know if he was coming "home" or not.

"I've thought about it a lot and not reached any positive conclusions," said Rachel. "I know a lot of bullshit goes down. Yet I'm putting up with it, and not really hating it."

What *was* she getting out of it, I wondered, since all she did was complain about his sloppy habits (Rachel is compulsively neat) and his spending most of their evenings together on the telephone.

"I think maybe Carl is a study to me," said Rachel. "Someone I cannot figure out. Someone who not only says he doesn't want a relationship, but really doesn't. I didn't believe him for a while, or thought enough of my ability to make him come round, but I must say for him that he told me where it was at right from the first."

Ah, yes! I dig you, but I must be free. But Carl was not honest enough to say, "No, I'm not going to move my cats and my stuff into your place." He's not above exploiting Rachel's hopes and illusions. No ties, but why not take advantage of the home comforts she has to offer?

And from Carl's point of view, why not indeed? It is, to a large extent, a question of supply and demand. When there are so many more women than men who are ravenous for romance . . . when smart, sensible women sleep with a guy once or twice and say, "Move in with me" . . . well then, something has to give. There are a lot of men who make it a practice to live the way Carl does. They like the woman, she's got a nice place. So they move into the ready-made nest and play house for a while . . . until they get bored or restless or find someone they like better. They have not helped to build the nest; they are not really involved or committed. Sometimes they contribute to household expenses. Quite often they don't.

Since this type of arrangement was designed to fill the vacuum that nature is said to abhor, it could well prove satisfactory to both parties, if only they would accept it for what it is. But the women are mostly anxious, insecure, and resentful. This is *not* what they want. And the men are foot-loose, alienated, and unsatisfied. Somehow, this isn't what they want either.

Manhood, as defined in our society, involves not only power but responsibility, obligation, and honor. Many men of liberationist persuasion, eager to escape the provider trap, are relinquishing responsibility along with power, unaware that they are also cutting themselves off from their identity as men. For as yet no adequate substitute definitions are available. And for most women, identity is still tied up with caring for a man . . . or a child. That is one reason for the trend to have babies without husbands. Having given birth, your woman-hood is proved once and for all.

And when you're in love, or living with a man, your wom-anhood is also safe, even if you're miserable. Both Rachel and Heather admit that the appeal of the man "with one foot out the door" is not just the challenge or the availability. He also allows the woman more control over her life. If, or rather *when* he leaves, it will hurt, but it will not destroy the fabric of her existence.

"Certain free-living women are apt to have trouble finding and holding on to satisfactory males," according to Doctors Ferdinand Lundberg and Marynia Farnham. Though their language and bias are grimly Freudian, the doctors give a fairly accurate description of some men's fear of women. "[Men] usually sense some lack of true tenderness [read: subservi-ence] about them. The egocentricity of the free-living woman disturbs them . . . they come to feel . . . that they are con-fronted with an adversary, a rival. . . . Unable to hold the fully masculine man, such a woman perforce falls back on the passive-feminine, juvenile, and even homosexual male."

Now the "passive-feminine" man is apt to be a very good lover—a far better lover, in fact, than the "fully masculine" man. Since the female aspect of his own nature is so strong, he "understands" women and knows exactly how to get around them. Such men are often the Don Juan type . . . unwilling or unable to engage in relationships of true mutuality and com-mitment, they will enter with impunity where other men fear to tread. If nothing else, Don Juan is sexually potent; he is only playing at the game of love and he's not afraid of the Big Bad Bitch . . . the specter of the Goddess has no hold over him. In any case, he can be had—even by the New Woman. And she may know what he is deep down, as they say, but beggars can't be choosers. What's more, beggars seem to have an almost limitless capacity to deceive themselves.

Even if the woman can understand the exigencies of the times and accept the man as he is, often the man cannot. He's got an image problem; he feels humiliated and deeply resents his dependent position. He tends to be spoiled, vain, selfish, deceitful (all the things women have been accused of being in the past). The woman, of course, needs someone she can, if not lean on, at least rely on once in a while—no goddess she. But she finds she is saddled with a pampered child, or a man whose behavior can best be described as "bitchy." She herself has spoiled him and he knows he can do whatever he likes.

What this type of man likes to do, much of the time, is get high. For years I've wondered why so many attractive, capable women fall in love with drunkards and junkies, men who are "on" something or other every moment of their waking day. Here's one clue: it feeds the female dream of the Beautiful Prince. If only the spell could be broken (by love, of course, what else?), if only he could cast off his ugly toad disguise (always the doing of some impersonal evil force like booze or dope) and emerge as the Beautiful Prince we just *know* dwells beneath, then we will love each other and live happily ever after. If a man has his life together and turns out not to be a Beautiful Prince but a male chauvinist pig, then the dream goes by the boards. And so we find it easier to love the losers, the also-rans, the ones with permanently jammed "potential." There are a lot of them around, for one thing, and if they are chronically drugged, dropped out, and unemployed . . . if they are childish and more than a little gay, so much the worse for us. At least our servitude is freely given, not demanded by an autocratic superior. If the unconscious element of contempt for the man's weakness makes us feel guilty, this causes us to dote on him even more. And the man who loves his drugs more than he loves his woman usually knows what's happening. His resentment is, in a sense, justified, for the woman's motives in taking up with him (often going so far as to get high with him, against her inclinations) are highly suspect.

Here's what typically happens in such a ménage: the woman goes out to work, often at some slave labor like office work or waitressing, while the man stays home and indulges in fantasies of writing, painting, playing music, or whatever else he pretends to be into aside from his *real* occupation, which is getting stoned. It is assumed that (a) menial jobs are easier to get for women, who can disguise their own unconventionality more easily (this is largely true); (b) such work is less devastating to the woman's psyche, since her "balls"— meaning pride, ego, integrity—are not at stake; and (c) a man's artistic efforts, no matter how inept, are always to be taken seriously, whereas a woman's creative endeavors, even when of obvious excellence, are always secondary to the more basic requirements—that she be attractive, compliant, good-natured, and above all, uncritical. She must not be a "bring-down," must never show what Joyce Carol Oates describes as "that touch of commonsense irony that loses us all our men."

Out in the communes and communities of the counterculture, where drug-taking is less virulent, the women have also assumed a deliberately marginal role. They cook and bake the bread even when the men don't work the land, and mostly they don't. The necessary cash usually comes from parents who are more loath to let daughters fend for themselves than sons.

Of course, women have always worked to support their men's artistic and intellectual efforts. Women throughout the ages, finding themselves married to drunkards, accepted their "widowhood" and went to work. It does seem odd, however, that there are so many of these relationships at a time when women are ostensibly emerging from oppression, and that men who are dropouts from the intellectual and spiritual life, as well as the conventional world, seem to have no trouble finding women who will support them, emotionally as well as financially.

Not that the women *like* it. They complain, they fret. But they put up with it. Whatever the price, they must have it—that special thrill, that quickening in the gut; love is the answer. . . . Even though we've forgotten the question. . . . Even though there really never *was* a question.

I talked about the dependent-lover problem with Lanie. At thirty-nine, with two divorces behind her, a boy of fourteen and a girl of seven to look after, and with her health and spirits seriously undermined by two operations, Lanie is still beautiful, with compelling green eyes and a mass of reddish hair. Witty, full of vitality, she has a gift for attracting people. Lanie has been a teacher, has written poetry and published a novel. Yet most of her life was given over to being a housewife and mother. A compulsive housekeeper, she would slide into the domestic trap with self-destructive relish. At the time we talked, she was having a love affair with a young musician, ten years her junior, and debating whether or not she should allow him to move in with her.

"I've been thinking about Chuck, and you know, he's really penniless. Now at the moment it is of no importance to me that I feed him and pay for movies and dinners out. . . ."

Lanie admitted, however, that it might well become important later on, especially if they lived together, for she is by no means rich. The tendency is to let it ride—why not, since there are no more rules? But as soon as the bloom is off the romance, or the man fails us in some way, the hidden resentment will out. He didn't come home when he was supposed to, and suddenly we are in a rage. He is taking unfair advantage; we are being ripped off.

What he's taking unfair advantage of is our yen for what Lanie calls the "Zap." "We go for the plumage," she says. "Man spreads his feathers and woman gets hung up on the feathers and discovers later that that's all there is . . . no substance. But I think you have to have it. It's the starting point, and without it, you have nothing at all. You can be the best of friends, but if there isn't that thing that says, *Zap! Look at that! I've got to have that! That's good!* then you have no basis for a relationship.

"The mating game has to be replaced with growth of some sort," Lanie agreed, "otherwise it dies. But the plumage—that's the energy force. The person has to be feeding you something. Look how beautiful the mind is . . . it can be an infinite storehouse. A lifetime isn't enough, if you've got the right person."

Here we get to the heart of the matter. The truth is, we do not often fall in love with the "right" person. The Zap is often triggered by someone who approximates some unconscious ideal—a parent, perhaps, or a movie star—someone who perpetuates a pattern that we, as adults, might want no part of. On one sexual-emotional level we tend to be drawn to opposites . . . to people who, as Anaïs Nin puts it, "act out for us a self we cannot and do not wish to act out." On another level of love, like friendship, we seek out people similar to ourselves. Here, the sexual-romantic fanfare may be missing . . . it may be someone we're not in the habit of being attracted by, "not our type," too much like ourselves to produce the tension, the electricity we associate with falling in love.

It is unfashionable to talk about the difference between attraction and love, or to introduce the quaint notion of a soul mate. Modern woman would be reluctant to admit that's what she's missing, as she leaps from affair to affair, getting no real satisfaction—she's not even sure there *is* such a thing as the soul. What's more, the sexual-emotional Zap is powerful. It cannot and should not be dismissed. Lanie believes the instinctive drawing toward someone is positive. "Though people are destructive, there is also the instinct for survival and people are turned on to someone who is right for them," she says. "But they destroy what it is in them they want. Your conditioning fucks it up. You cannot help being attracted, and you cannot keep yourself from destroying."

Lanie and I have been friends for years; we know that we share a tendency to be attracted to men of dark, demonic natures—men who possess a kind of Dionysian energy that charges us. It may be that these men do something important for our psyches, that they represent unassimilated aspects of ourselves, a yearning for chaos and irresponsibility, for living at the edge, where the perceptions are more real. Where our conditioning "fucks it up" is that we immediately seek to get ourselves into a domestic situation with these men. We have a basic need for order and stability and so we try to make these men truthful, honorable, reliable—all the things they are not. When they refuse, we are indignant and distraught. Obviously, if we are going to be drawn to such men, for perhaps sound psychological reasons, we have to forget about living with them and domesticating them, about expecting anything other than the connection of the moment.

"I thought of tying in with Chuck because he has this energy," said Lanie, "but then maybe I shouldn't be with him at this stage of my life, when I need mellowing, not more excitement."

Even if it were possible to give up on the excitement of the Zap, it would not seem worthwhile to many people. Like Lanie, they will continue to act out the cycle: attraction, approach-avoidance, rejection, pain, disappointment. I can only suggest to these people that they try to maintain some degree of inner detachment, even self-mockery, throughout these gyrations.

One way is to look at the pattern very closely, and when a lover you discover at the gate, my friend, do take a second look. You may find he is remarkably like your exes—Tom, Dick, and Harry. The "blindness" of love is largely self-imposed. If you can see him clearly and still want to take a chance on love, then do so with an awareness of the risks, and if things don't work out well, don't rail against your fate, the treachery of men, or even your analyst, who has still not cured you of your neuroses.

Most people have no very clear idea of what they are looking for in a mate. They wait for the magical Zap, and when it happens, that's it! That's the given, the raw material you have to "work" with. Love conquers all! But even if we do know what we want and need, we may have to face the fact that we may not be able to get it. There is, for the New Woman, an indisputable shortage of comparable men. So, we have to ask ourselves if we are willing and able to make the necessary compromises, accept provisional situations, consent to share love with men who are not our ideals. And if we cannot, we should be prepared to do without.

There is another kind of man with whom modern woman can find romance, provided she is able to make certain psychic adjustments. Julie Baumgold calls him the "blue-collar lover." One of the little ironies to come out of women's lib is a strong, if largely unacknowledged, fascination with the totally unreconstructed, animalistic, supermasculine male. Call it nostalgia. Call it desperation. These men have the appeal of the exotic, the forbidden . . . the endangered wild species. The *macho* construction worker is not troubled by the New Impotence. He has a very clear idea of what it means to be a man. To him, the liberated woman is, first of all, a woman. He may be impressed, even proud of her, but he is not competing and therefore not threatened. How can he be in awe of her when he fucks her every night and she moans and begs for more? (Of course, the mere fact that he fucks her makes her a little contemptible.)

This could work out very well, in theory. In practice, the woman usually cannot resist tampering with the natural man, trying to improve him—teaching him how to dress, how to order in restaurants. The woman's ego is involved. If these men are brought out of the closet and accepted as lovers, then one is responsible for them in the eyes of the world. One may know their true worth, the simple honest goodness of them, but what will one's friends say? Once the woman has succeeded in refining her primitive, he may lose his appeal for her, and what is worse, she may lose all her appeal for him.

It is not that easy for a woman to give up her dream of a true mate, an equal and a partner, a man she can wholeheartedly admire. Her blue-collar lover may give her what she needs for a while—sex and affection and loyalty—her batteries may be recharged, but she is not satisfied. Always, it is the compromise, the second-best, which humiliates and breaks the heart.

Renata believes she could make the compromise without undue strain. A fortyish brunette, with sensitive features and

---

dynamic good looks, she is a writer, editor, and cosmopolite who has lived and loved in New York, Paris, London, and California. She was married and divorced years ago, and has lived with a number of men since. The public Renata is witty, sophisticated, and knows her way around. The private Renata, whom she described as "neurotic but sober," reveals herself in the note of urgency, of controlled desperation, beneath the calm, intelligent voice.

"While our need is to be with someone whose interests are similar to our own, someone we can have a dialogue with, *their* need is not to be with us and they invariably choose another kind of woman," said Renata. "I've been aware of this for a long time, and I must tell you that I no longer need to be with a peer if there are other qualities that interest me . . . like a certain approach to nature, a certain way of dealing with existence. These are powerful attributes and a fisherman could have them—or someone who works for the electric company. But in our classless society we tend to get involved with chic and lifestyles so that we're not really leading inventive or imaginative lives."

What she means is that it's difficult to *meet* a fisherman. But Renata is quite prepared to go off to New Zealand, or someplace like that, where she thinks there might be possibilities of lovers, if not mates. I expressed some doubt that she would really drop her life, her friends, and go live in some fishing village in New Zealand. "Oh, I'm due for some heavy traveling," said Renata. "My brain tells me I shouldn't, out of some loyalty to some abstraction. But my cunt says, do it!"

What about her heart? It was with the cunt at the moment, she said. I predicted she'd be climbing the walls in six months if she did go to New Zealand. "Fine," she said, "I'll come back then."

We went on to talk about why women seemed to need a peer and men did not—their women did not have to be "suitable" if they provided warmth and comfort, food and sex. "A man will rarely leave a woman because there's no longer any reason to be with her," said Renata. "He will leave only for someone to replace her. Men who are *into* relationships with women will not live alone for a moment. Whereas a woman will live alone rather than with someone she's not attuned to. Women are braver, they are purer emotionally, more striving in what they want."

It may be that men feel more complete in themselves. It may also be that men feel more alienated, more alone, and that, unlike women, they have accepted this as the human condition. For despite the fact that women are so pure and striving emotionally, they are selling out like crazy, and it is definitely a buyer's market. I asked Renata how she would feel if she had to spend the rest of her life without a mate.

"I've been confronted with that possibility," she replied, "and yes, I'd do *anything*. I don't want to live alone. Yes, I've thought about making it with another woman. But there's a continuity, a verticality that happens with the other sex . . . the woman thing is inward, a form of narcissism, and some women prefer that. But I'm attracted to men—it's an enormous force in my life."

The addiction to love-sex cannot be reasoned away. It can only be repressed, or transcended. A cause or religion might do it, but a career is not likely to, and neither are children. Even a steady, unromantic husband doesn't always help— married women are notoriously prone to this vague ache and yearning. It seems the craving has been injected into us at so early an age, in such concentrated doses, that if we are deprived for any length of time we begin to wither, to die inside. Rather than that we will do *anything* . . . even for the precarious "freshening" that a night of good sex can bring . . . even for the temporary reassurance that a night of uninspired or failed sex can bring, provided there is some warmth of touch, some affection.

But a night in bed often brings neither freshening nor reassurance, only more confusion, greater longing. So after a while you decide, no more of that! Screwing around is a bummer; it messes up your mind and your body responses. There's this hole in your soul, and no amount of cock is going to fill it.

What happens then is that you spend a lot of time lying around in a funk, concocting endless romantic-erotic daydreams, the way you did when you were a kid. The contents of my own fantasies have changed considerably since I was fourteen, but their essential nature hasn't: in them I strive to play the Great Game so beautifully, so truly, that nobody loses. My partner and I surmount all the pitfalls, triumph over all the demons, and stay in sync all the time—not glued together, olden Tango-style, but watching each other, taking cues from each other, adding to one another's dance. These fancies come upon me like attacks of flu, leaving me drained and lethargic and depressed. Doctor, I have this recurrent dream: I shall find someone to love and live happily ever after!

It is in the nature of love, and even of pleasure, that when they are pursued simply for their own sake, they will fail to provide full satisfaction. Only when attraction is not based exclusively on the "what can you do for me" principle, but on a common purpose that transcends the relationship itself, is there any hope it will grow into enduring love.

At one time, the raising of children, the demands of family and clan provided strong enough cement to bind a couple together—that and the weight of the belief that marriage was for life. Today, children are a personal indulgence rather than a necessity for survival; consequently, they tend to be a liability in a love relationship. A better common purpose is work—M. and Mme. Curie come to mind, or more recently, Masters and Johnson. The best examples for me, because they are not married or even living together but have loved each other for over twenty-five years, are Simone de Beauvoir and Jean-Paul Sartre.

Love seems to work best when it is a by-product of something else—dedication to a cause, a belief, even a new life-style. Having some other primary goal, we need not then make such heavy demands on love. For when we *must* have something, we are already in trouble.

As money comes easily to the rich, so love comes more easily to those who are not forever seeking it, who give off those ineffable vibes of self-containment, which have nothing to do with the outward trappings of liberation and cannot be faked. "Clutching is the surest way to murder love," says May Sarton, "as if it were a kitten, not to be squeezed so hard, or a flower to fade in a tight hand."

To live in a state of love is not easy, with someone forever inside your head, monitoring every move. "Will he like the new dress I'm thinking of buying?" An incident in the street gets rehearsed into instant anecdote, to dish up to your loved one at home. Some call that sharing, the supreme happiness of love. And some women would rather do something because Joe, who's a shit, *doesn't* like it, than because they want to. But for many others this kind of possession is a hardship—it doesn't allow enough inner space for the personality to unfold according to its natural bent. For many women the great need for love is pitted against a growing impatience, an increasing intolerance for all the mind-fucking that goes on in the name of love.

The problem lies in the phenomenon of love itself and cannot be blamed on the war between the sexes. This conclusion was borne out by the homosexuals I talked with. They seem to have just as much trouble with love as anyone else—perhaps more, for they have even less tradition and place even greater weight on the affair as an end in itself. Though they all had careers, mostly in the arts, these homosexuals, both male and female, admitted to the whole "rejoicing unto heaven, sad unto death" trip, depending on the moods of the loved one, and to feeling incomplete without that special someone to care for. Homosexual men, unlike straight men, tend to be as hung up on love as women are.

Admittedly, it is difficult to care, but not too much—to stay open and potent in loving and at the same time maintain one's own center, an inner composure, and to let go when the time comes, with grace and dignity: to let the hurt wash over us without resisting, so it will pass more quickly, and not take it so *personally* . . . to remember that *everybody,* regardless of merit, has been hurt, rejected, betrayed—Christ and Cleopatra and even Elizabeth Taylor. The death of love is painful, but it can be borne without shame, humiliation, or self-loathing, if we can deprogram ourselves from the wounded-ego bit: "How dare he do this to me?" Or the other side of the coin, self-pity: "Why are guys *always* doing this to me?" Most of our woes come from being unable to accept things as they really are, from seeing things only as they *ought* to be. What if, in our secret hearts, we are relieved to be rid of the creep and know it's the best thing that could have happened? He *jilted* us, didn't he? So we respond with Pavlovian reflex pain, unable to accept that we cannot lose what we never possessed. So simple, and yet so hard to let go . . . of hate if it cannot be love; for hate, too, is a bond and a connection.

People tell me, smiling a little defensively, that I am pessimistic. In terms of the accepted views of how relations between men and women *should* be—either according to traditional concepts or the radical-revolutionary bias of the moment—I am indeed pessimistic about real-life people ever fitting into those narrow slots. But I am optimistic about the possibility of revising our attitudes and our goals; of sharpening our awareness so that we may free ourselves of destructive habits of attraction and perception. I even believe it is possible to learn to enjoy the variety and complexity, the irrational, unpredictable, and *funny* things that can happen between human beings involved in the explosive combinations, or permutations, of love and sex. It is useless to paint a utopian picture of liberation. Real freedom is an inner condition, and it involves a day-to-day struggle. But that struggle can be creative, full of exciting new possibilities.

"The serious problems of life are never fully solved," said Carl Gustav Jung. "If they should appear to be so it is a sure sign that something has been lost. The meaning and purpose of a problem seem to lie not in its solution but in our working on it incessantly. This alone prevents us from stultification and putrefaction." The striving toward growth and development must be directed not toward changing events—"working" on a relationship, or making a partner "come round"—but toward changing our own demands and expectations. The problems of love and loneliness may never be solved, but we may perhaps learn to deal with them, without despair—or undue hope.

Anaïs Nin
IN FAVOR OF THE SENSITIVE MAN

This last year I spent most of my time with young women in colleges, young women doing their Ph.D.'s on my work. The talk about the diaries always leads to private and intimate talks about their lives. I became aware that the ideals, fantasies, and desires of these women were going through a transition. Intelligent, gifted, participating in the creativity and activities of their time in history, they seemed to have transcended the attraction for the conventional definition of a man.

It was no longer the purely *macho* type they had learned to expose as false masculinity, its outer aspects only, physical force, dexterity in games, muscles, arrogance, but more dangerous still, lacking in sensitivity, in lyricism, in the capacity to love, in inner qualities. The hero of *Last Tango in Paris* repulsed them. The sadist, the man who humiliates woman, whose show of power is a façade. The so-called heroes, the stance of a Hemingway or a Mailer in writing, the false strength. All of this was exposed, disposed of by these new women, too intelligent to be deceived, too wise and too proud to be subjected to this show of power which did not protect them (as former generations of women believed) but endangered their existence as individuals.

The attraction shifted to the poet, the musician, the singer, the sensitive man they had studied with, to the natural, sincere man without stance or display, nonassertive, the one concerned with true values, not ambition, the one who hated war and greed, commercialism and political expediencies. A new type of man to match the new type of woman. They helped each other through college, they answered each other's poems, they wrote confessional and self-examining letters, they prized relationship, they gave care to it, time, attention. They did not like impersonal sensuality. Both wanted to work at something they loved.

I met many couples which fitted this description. Neither one dominated. Each one worked at what he did best, shared labors, unobtrusively, without need to establish roles or boundaries. The characteristic trait was gentleness. There was no head of the house. There was no need to assert which one was the supplier of income. They had learned the subtle art of oscillation, which is human. Neither strength nor weakness are fixed qualities. We all have our days of strength and our days of weakness. They had learned rhythm, suppleness, relativity. Each had knowledge and special intuitions to contribute. There is no war of the sexes between these couples. There is no need to draw up contracts on the rules of marriage. Most of them do not feel the need to marry. Some want children and some do not. They are equally aware of the function of dreams—not as symptoms of neurosis, but as guidance to our secret nature. They know that each is endowed with both masculine and feminine qualities.

A few of these young women displayed a new anxiety. It was as though having lived so long under the direct or indirect domination of man (setting the style of their life, the pattern, the duties) they had become accustomed to it, and now that it was gone, that they were free to make decisions, to be mobile, to speak their wishes, to direct their own lives, they felt like a ship without a rudder. I saw questions in their eyes. Was sensitivity felt as overgentle? Permissiveness as weakness? They missed authority, the very thing they had struggled to overcome. The old groove had functioned for so long. Women as dependents. A few women independent, but few in proportion to the dependent ones. The offer of total love was unusual. A love without egocentricity, without exigencies, without moral strictures. A love which did not define the duties of women (you must do this and that, you must help me with my work, you must entertain and further my career).

A love which was almost a twinship. No potentates, no dictators, no head of the house. Strange. It was new. It was a new country. You cannot have independence and dependence. You can alternate them equally, and then both can grow, unhampered, without obstacles. This sensitive man is aware of woman's needs. He seeks to let her be. But a few women are uneasy, not recognizing that the elements they are missing are those which thwarted woman's expansion, her testing of her gifts, her mobility, her development. They mistake sensitivity for weakness. Perhaps because the sensitive man lacks the aggressivity of the *macho* man (which sent him hurtling through business and politics at tragic cost to family and personal relationships.)

I met a young man who, although the head of a business by inheritance, did not expect his wife to serve the company, to entertain people not attractive to her, to assist in his contacts. She was free to pursue her own interests, which lay in psychology and training welfare workers. She became anxious that the two different sets of friends, his business associates and her psychologists, would create totally separate lives and estrange them. It took her a while to observe that her psychological experiences were serving his interests in another way. He was learning to handle those who worked for him in a more humanistic way. When an employee was found cheating while pumping the company's gas to the other employees, he called him in and obtained his life history. He discovered the reason for the cheating (high hospital bills for a child) and remedied it instead of firing him, thus winning a loyal employee from then on. Interests which seemed at first divergent became interdependent.

Another couple decided that, both being writers, one would teach one year and leave the other free to write, and the other would take on teaching the next year. The husband was already a fairly well-known writer. The wife had only published poems in magazines so far, but was preparing a book of criticism. It was her turn to teach. He found himself invited as a faculty member's husband and was asked at parties: "Do you also write?" The situation could have caused friction. The wife remedied it by having reprinted in the school paper a review of the husband's last novel, which established his standing.

Young women are engaging in political action when young men are withdrawing because of disillusionment. And the new woman is winning new battles. The fact that certain laws were changed renewed the faith of the new man. Women in politics are still at the stage of David and Goliath. They believe in the effect of a single stone! Their faith is invigorating when the couple are in sympathetic vibes, as they call it.

The old situation of the man obsessed with business, whose life was shortened by stress, and whose life ended at retirement, was reversed by a young wife who encouraged his hobby—painting, so that he retired earlier because of his interest in painting and travel.

In these situations the art of coordination manifests itself, rather than the immature emphasis on irreconcilable differences. With maturity comes the sense that activities are interrelated and nourish each other.

Another source of bewilderment for the new woman is that many of the new men do not have the old ambitions. They do not want to spend their lives in the pursuit of a fortune. They want to travel while they are young, live in the present. I met them hitchhiking in Greece, Spain, Italy, France. They were living entirely in the present and accepting the hardships for the sake of the present adventures. One young woman felt physically unfit for the difficulties and carried a lot of vitamins in her one-and-only pack. She told me: "At first he made fun of me, but then he understood I was not sure I could take the trip physically, and he became as protective as possible. If I had married a conventional man, his concept of protection would have been to keep me home. I would not have enjoyed all these marvels I have discovered with David, who challenged my strength and made me stronger for it." Neither one thought of surrendering the dream of travel while young.

One of the most frequent questions young women ask me is: How can a woman create a life of her own, an atmosphere of her own when her husband's profession dictates their lifestyle? If he is a doctor, a lawyer, a psychologist, a teacher, the place they live in, the stereotyping, the demands of the neighbors, all set the pattern of life.

Judy Chicago, the well-known painter and teacher, made a study of women painters and found that whereas the men painters all had studios separate from the house, the women did not, and painted either in the kitchen or some spare room.

But many young women have taken literally Virginia Woolf's *A Room of One's Own* and rented studios away from the family. One couple, who lived in a one-room house, set up a tent on the terrace for the wife's writing activities. The very feeling of "going to work," the physical act of detachment, the sense of value given to the work by isolating it, became a stimulant and a help. To create another life, they found, was not a breaking away or separating. It is striking that for woman, any break or separation carries with it an aura of loss, as if the symbolic umbilical cord still affected all her emotional life and each act were a threat to unity and ties.

This fear is in women, not in men, but it was learned from men. Men, led by their ambitions, did separate from their families, were less present for the children, were absorbed, submerged by their professions. But this happened to men and does not necessarily have to happen to women. The unbroken tie lies in the feelings. It is not the hours spent with husband or children that are important, but the quality and completeness of the presence. Men are often physically present and mentally preoccupied. Woman is more capable of turning away from her work to give full attention to a weary husband or a child's scratched finger.

If women have witnessed the father "going away" because of his work, they will retain anxiety about their own "going away" to meetings, conferences, lectures, or other professional commitments.

For the new woman and the new man, the art of connecting and relating separate interests will be a challenge. If women today do not want a nonexistent husband married to Big Business, they will accept a simpler form of life to have the enjoyment of a husband whose life blood has not been sucked by big companies. I see the new woman shedding many luxuries. I love to see them, simply dressed, relaxed, natural, playing no roles. For the transitional stage was woman's delicate problem: how to pass from being submerged and losing her identity in a relationship, how to learn to merge without loss of self. The new man is helping by his willingness to change too, from rigidities to suppleness, from tightness to openness, from uncomfortable roles to the relaxation of no roles.

One young woman was offered a temporary teaching job away from home. The couple had no children. The young husband said: "Go ahead if that is what you want to do." If he had opposed the plan, which added to her teaching credits, she would have resented it. But because he let her go, she felt he did not love her deeply enough to hold on to her. She left with a feeling of being deserted, while he felt her leaving also as a desertion. These feelings lay below the conscious acceptance. The four months separation might have caused a break. But the difference is that they were willing to discuss these feelings, to laugh at their ambivalence and contradictions.

If in the unconscious there still lie reactions we cannot control, at least we can prevent them from doing harm to the present situation. If both were unconsciously susceptible to the fear of being "deserted," they had to find a way to grow independent from a childhood pattern. Otherwise, enslaved by childhood fears, neither one could move from the house. In exposing them they were able to laugh at the inconsistency of wanting freedom and yet wanting the other to hold on.

Very often in the emerging new woman, the assertion of differences carries too heavy an indication of dissonances, disharmony; but it is a matter of finding the relation, as we are finding the relation between art and science, science and psychology, religion and science. It is not similarities which create harmony, but the art of fusing various elements which enrich life. Professional activities tend to demand almost too much concentration; this becomes a narrowing of experience for each one. The infusion of new currents of thoughts, stretching the range of interests, is beneficial to both.

Perhaps some new women and new men fear adventure and change. The life of Margaret Mead indicates that she sought the man involved in the same passionate devotion to archeology, but the result was that the husband studied the legends, the myths of the tribe, and she was left to study childbirth and the raising of children. So a common interest does not necessarily mean equality.

All of us carry seeds of anxieties left from childhood, but the determination to live with others in close and loving harmony can overcome all the obstacles provided we have learned to *integrate the differences.*

Watching these young couples and how they resolve the problems of new attitudes, new consciousness, I feel we might be approaching a humanistic era in which differences and inequalities may be resolved without war.

Yoko Ono proposed the "feminization of society. The use of feminine tendencies as a positive force to change the world. . . . We can evolve rather than revolt."

The empathy these new men show woman is born of their acceptance of their own emotional, intuitive, sensory, and humanistic approach to relationships. They allow themselves to weep (men never wept), to show vulnerability, to expose their fantasies, share their inmost selves. Some women are baffled by the new regime. They have not yet recognized that to have empathy one must to some extent feel what the other feels. That means that if woman is to assert her creativity or her gifts, the man has to assert his own crucial dislike of what was expected of him in the past.

The new type of young man I have met is exceptionally fitted for the new woman, but she is not yet totally apprecia-tive of his tenderness, his growing proximity to woman, his attitude of twinship rather than differentiation. People who once lived under a dictatorship often are at a loss to govern themselves. This loss is a transitional one: it may mean the beginning of a totally new life and freedom. The man is there. He is an equal. He treats you like an equal. In moments of uncertainty you can still discuss problems with him you could not have talked about twenty years ago. Do not, I say to today's women, please do not mistake sensitivity for weak-ness. This was the mistake which almost doomed our culture. Violence was mistaken for power, the misuse of power for strength. The subjection is still true in films, in the theater, in the media. I wanted the hero of *Last Tango in Paris* to die immediately. He was only destroyed at the end! The time span of a film. Will it take women as long to recognize sadism,

---

arrogance, tyranny, reflected so plainly in the world outside, in war and political corruption? Let us start the new regime of honesty, of trust, abolishment of false roles in our personal relationships, and it will eventually affect the world's history as well as women's development.

Donald Barthelme
THE BILL

When the affair was over, at long last, I presented her with the bill. She reached out a hand lightly dusted with not unappealing pale-pink blotches and took the bill. She began reading the bill, which was three pages long, for we had been many months together. At length she pointed a finger at an item in the middle of page two and said: "Four dollars and seventy-five cents for toothpaste?"

"I have been conservative," I said. "Whenever there was a doubtful or nice question, I resolved the matter in your favor. During our time together you probably consumed something more like *five* dollars worth of toothpaste. The figure is based upon an estimated 240-odd brushings."

"Sometimes we stayed at my place," she said. "We used *my* toothpaste."

"I have allowed for that," I said. "My use of your toothpaste has been subtracted from your use of my toothpaste." Well did I remember the nights in her too-narrow bed. The mattress kept slipping off the bed proper, because of some engineering fault, and there was always the feeling of being "on the edge," a feeling incompatible with soft sleep and languorous, conflict-resolving dreams. Consequently, nights at her place had been infrequent.

Her eye, that eye that I had once peered into, along with its mate, with an avidity not to be believed, finding there promises that I was not such a bad fellow after all, no matter what was being said about me in the agora, on the bush telegraph, in the *Progressive Grocer,* lay for a moment longer on the "toothpaste" entry and then continued down the list.

"Storage," she said. "What is 'storage'?"

"Very little, as I remember. Three dollars, isn't it?"

"Yes," she said, "three dollars, but for what?"

"Was there not folded, in my chest of drawers, for the period in question, an orange and blue bathrobe?"

She admitted with a grimace that the bathrobe had indeed remained in the chest of drawers for the period in question. I watched her forehead, behind which her reasoning processes romped and rioted; it was clear that she was calculating what the cleaners would have asked had she hung the bathrobe there, in a plastic bag, in a mothproof vault, and concluding that the charge was not unjust.

"Meals," she went on. "Twenty-four hundred and forty-nine dollars and forty-nine cents. Isn't that a bit on the stiff side?"

"It includes coffee in the mornings," I said. "Have you forgotten coffee in the mornings, on a silver tray?" For indeed it was thus that I had brought it to her, on a silver tray, with separate little pots for cream and sugar, and the occasional English muffin, with a bit of rose-hip jam on special occasions, such as my birthday. For the English muffins I had not billed her; the English muffins were, in terms of the bill, sheer gravy, a thing I did not mention out of a natural modesty and sweetness of character.

"Room!" she read. "You're charging me for the room on the nights we lay together, locked in the throes of love?"

One cannot be locked in a throe: on the contrary, the word implies movement, struggle, even abandon, but I let it pass.

"Only your half," I answered. "Any hotel in the world would class it as a double and price it accordingly. I am treating it as a single and the saving to you is considerable."

She was now tracing the figures with a gold pencil and employing as well a pocket electronic calculator of the type the Japanese fabricate so skillfully. The stylized numbers skittered in green across the window of the calculator.

"Four hundred and forty-eight dollars for brandy?"

"My love, you do like your little hit, before bed," I reminded her. "And Rémy Martin is now thirteen-and-a-half the bottle." Although she was in form a trifle twiggy, she had a great gullet, a truth she did not like to have recalled to her.

"Telephone calls," she read. "Gas, electricity——"

"Prorated," I said hurriedly. "Only *your share*."

"Books, newspapers, slides and filmstrips——"

"I had to educate myself in your area of specialization. To make myself knowledgeable and interesting. An expense I would not otherwise have incurred."

"Plays, concerts, films, places of amusement, cab fare—why is the cab-fare bit so big?"

"We went many times to the Botanical Garden," I said, "caressing each other under the pronghorn azalea, meanwhile keeping a sharp lookout for puritanical tree-keepers. Have you forgotten so soon? Did the azalea afternoons mean nothing to you?"

But she was concentrating on the bill.

"Medical," she said.

"My Equanil," I said.

"You're charging *me* for *your* Equanil?"

"Before I met you, I had no need of it."

"Sweets, cotton candy, popcorn, phonograph records, plants—I don't remember any plants."

"The cactus."

"The cactus died."

"Is that my fault? You didn't water it."

"I'm supposed to pay for a dead cactus?"

I started to reply, but her gaze had already been trapped by something further down the line. "Towels?" she said with an odd inflection. "Towels? Towels? *Towels?*"

"The laundromat people are in business just like anybody else."

With a shriek she seized from the wall my ornamental Khyber dagger, used by the Afridi mercenaries while guarding the Khyber Pass during the Afghan wars, and plunged it into my right side. I fell to the floor, writhing appropriately.

No matter. I am out of the intensive Care Unit now, comfortably settled in a semiprivate room with a pleasant view of the latest printout from the hospital computer. It is full of intriguing notations (03/27 LABORATORY 0212021 35.00) which I am studying with care. When I am discharged, I will put it all on the bill. One must pay for what one gets in this world, and I see no reason why the joy of cutting up an ex-lover should be exempted from this extremely sensible law of life.

Lois Gould
PORNOGRAPHY FOR WOMEN

The hand-lettered cardboard sign, posted outside a new peep-show parlor in Manhattan's fashionable East 50's, bore the usual enticing message: ADULTS ONLY. Underneath, in smaller, cruder letters, the management had scrawled what it considered a liberated afterthought: *Women Also Welcome.*

Now why in the name of male bonding would a smart young smut peddler with a choice midtown location want to let *women* in? Imagine it: Women riffling through his pile of $10 imported bondage magazines as if they were so many striped percales at a January white sale. Women snooping around his notions counter, giggling at the plastic "love aids." Women hogging the 30 Moviolas 30, elbowing the male regulars out of the way and popping their hot perfumed quarters into the slots for a quick peek at *Torture Chamber* and *Young Girl Does It with Very Old Guy.* Women asking for their money back if not completely satisfied. Women Also *Welcome?*

Sexism aside, it was clearly a sign of the times. The pornography industry, solemn protector and leering nurturer of man's most secret and profane sex life, is suddenly trying—with all the fumbling urgency of an adolescent lover—to go coed.

It was probably inevitable. Once blue movies such as *I Am Curious (Yellow)* and *Deep Throat* became a shockingly respectable, if not boringly chic, diversion for sophisticated mixed audiences; once frontal male nudity flashed success-fully on and off Broadway; once Marlon Brando talked dirty and performed simulated sex acts in a major box-office, $5, reserved-seat hit, it looked as if women were finally ready for "porn" and "porn" was more than ready for us.

Pornography—for either sex—has been defined as whatever turns the Supreme Court on. More seriously, the word is generally applied to the explicit depiction, in books, films or photographs, of sexual organs and sexual acts, in a manner designed to elicit a strong erotic response in the reader or viewer. The word itself derives from Greek terms that mean writing about harlots—thus, any graphic representation of illicit sexual material.

Some social scientists have observed that all societies need pornography—and also need to suppress it, since, like prostitution, it is an outlet for all the sexual feelings that are otherwise socially unacceptable. But, historically, men have been the primary consumers—as well as the pushers—of both pornography and prostitution. The reason, it has been suggested, is that these industries both reflect and reinforce the social "norm" of men as the sexual users and abusers of women. Thus, even voyeurism—intense erotic interest in watching other people's sexual behavior, a trait on which pornography feeds—has been a traditionally male phenomenon; psychiatrists have encountered few peeping tomboys among adult women.

The pendulum, however, is beginning to swing.

Though no one has yet dubbed them "boyie" magazines, the past year has brought us at least three slick, fun-and-gamy publications designed to do for women what *Playboy* and *Penthouse* presumably do for men. *Viva, Playgirl* and *Foxylady* all feature male nude pinups—centerfolded, coyly posed and genitally exposed—plus a dizzying assortment of titillating articles and advice on sex-related topics: Pubic hair styles *(Viva),* how to use a bidet *(Foxylady)* and why orgasmic women should be kinder to premature ejaculators *(Playgirl).*

Besides the magazines, there are books that reveal women's secret erotic fantasies, and X-rated movies whose ads, aimed at a mixed audience, attempt to soothe nagging female guilt feelings about enjoying voyeurism with the menfolk. Two recent instances: "Lets you feel good without feeling bad" *(Emmanuelle)* and "The first sex film about love" *(Wet Rainbow).*

So far, however, women haven't quite warmed to the subject. *Viva* magazine lost $3 million on its first 12 issues, though its publisher, Bob Guccione, who also publishes *Penthouse,* recently declared that *Viva* has been "marginally in the black" since last fall.

Some women who read these magazines protest that they do so *despite* the male nude pinups, which they find either silly or irritating—not sexy. Are they lying? Or merely repressed? Are they secretly turned on but not admitting it to themselves? Are younger women more stimulated than older ones?

The answer is some or all of the above. Many women do lie about their sexual response; they always have. Only the content of the lie changes from one generation to the next—from the Victorian woman denying *all* response to the loving wife faking orgasm to please her man. What a woman *says* she feels—indeed, what she may very well *think* she feels—still depends to a dismaying extent on what the dominant (male) culture expects of her at the moment.

Psychiatrist Mary Jane Sherfey has described this phenomenon as a persistent problem in research about female sexual response: "One wonders if this well-known difficulty women have in reporting their sexual sensations does not stem from the fact that they deceive themselves and us about the nature of these feelings because they are afraid that what they do feel is not what they *should* feel."

This year, what some women may think they "should" feel is sexually liberated. But by whose standard? They have been told they "should" take their multiple orgasm where they find it, and let the meaningful relationships fall where they may. When in doubt, they "should" turn on to their vibrators for quick release from the tensions of interpersonal sex. They "should" also rise above their fear of flying, hang up their hangups about needing love and/or a half-hour of foreplay, and, finally, buy matching his-and-hers pornography for the bathroom magazine rack.

If it all sounds like the plot of some well-thumbed male erotic fantasy, it is no wonder. Drs. Phyllis and Eberhard Kronhausen, the wife-and-husband team of psychoanalysts who study pornography laws, were onto this plot back in 1959: "In keeping with the [male] wish-fulfilling nature of obscene writings, the female characters . . . are just what men would like women to be: highly passionate, sensuous and sexually insatiable creatures who like nothing better than almost continuous intercourse.''

Classic porn always described men in a satyriasis-like condition of permanent sexual excitement, the Kronhausens observed. And the women in classic porn stories were perpetually "on the prowl for a new sexual partner, or a new sexual experience.''

But if the "new porn" for women is really men's sexual fantasies warmed over; if it offers, in fact, no truer picture of women's erotic desires than *The Confessions of Lady Beatrice,* then why is the stuff selling at all?

Rumor has it that much of the women's sex-magazine readership is actually made up of male homosexuals, because they, at least, find the male nudes sexy. When a character in *The Ritz,* a new Broadway comedy set in a gay steam bath, exclaims, "I *hope* I don't *need* this month's *Viva!",* the line gets a big, knowledgeable laugh.

Many women, especially young, liberation-hungry women, buy one or two issues out of curiosity, or go to a porno movie whose 22-year-old female star gives interviews saying she got into the business because porno movies excited *her* sexually. Thousands of women will read another woman's book whose heroine pursues erotic equal rights by what used to be called sleeping around. But when the novelty of such "new" notions about female sexuality wears off, women in general don't get "turned on."

Why not?

I talked to a number of women about the pictures in *Viva* and *Playgirl.* These were typical reactions: "Maybe I'd like them better if the men looked more masculine"; "Maybe if the penises were erect"; "Maybe if the poses were more *erotic.*" Maybe. Women who have seen male homosexual pinup magazines describe those photographs as somehow more sensual and appealing than the ones in *Viva* or *Playgirl,* if only because it is evident that the photographer, model and magazine editors all think of the male body as an erotic object—and know how to present it as such.

Still another complaint by women who are turned off, rather than on, by the *Viva-Playgirl* male nudies is that where a naked couple appear in an erotic "photo-essay," the two never seem remotely like lovers. The pictures often have a soft-focus romantic-dream quality, but, as one woman put it, "there's no sexual tension." Nakedness is not enough.

Neither, it seems, is naked sex in action, as in the peep-show parlors which show what one male film critic calls "industrial documentaries"—piston-and-pump genitals doing their thing—or the new crop of X-rated "sexploitation" movies aimed at middle-class mixed audiences. Though, again, curiosity—or a nagging husband—may propel a woman to go once or twice to a *Deep Throat* or *Behind the Green Door,* the experience rarely makes a hardcore fan of her. The lines outside *Emmanuelle,* a recent hit at a classy midtown-Manhattan theater, were still overwhelmingly male.

Molly Haskell, a film critic and author of *From Reverence to Rape,* a study of women's treatment in the movies, believes that what is missing for women in the typical porno flick is the same ingredient left out of the women's sex magazines: believable sexual tension between the man and woman. There is no seduction, virtually no romantic suspense, and only perfunctory foreplay (kissing, caressing, sensual interaction). Women moviegoers, says Ms. Haskell, are "profoundly aroused by observing the total man-woman relationship", they are much *less* stimulated by watching narrow-focus genital contact, which is, of course, the essential core—whether hard, soft or medium—of the blue movie.

Some women felt cheated after seeing *Last Tango in Paris,* because Brando never took off his clothes. But many others responded strongly to the eroticism portrayed in *Tango,* because they were already turned on to Brando. In fact, some women have said they would have been less aroused by the sight of a nude Brando whose body failed to match the Adonis in their Brando fantasies.

To many sex researchers, women's lack of response to the "new porn" comes as no surprise. After all, American Women have, technically, always been "also welcome" to buy, read, collect and be erotically stimulated by pornographic material.

Books, pictures and films depicting male nude genitals and sexual acts have been more or less freely available to any woman willing to ask for them—under the counter, through the mail in plain brown wrapper, at seedy stag-movie houses or in the private collections of male *aficionados* willing to share. Yet few women ever bothered to ask for such material and, until recently, few men thought they ever would. It had been widely believed, by pornographers, by experts on sexual behavior, and by both men and women in general, that women were somehow biologically immune to porn; that their lack of pleasurable response to "dirty" books and pictures was a permanent condition of their peculiar sexual character.

In 1953, the Kinsey report, *Sexual Behavior in the Human Female,* presented impressive statistical data supporting the view that a woman could not be sexually aroused by seeing pictures of nude bodies, or even by seeing a man's genitals in the flesh. Any man who attempted to excite his female partner by showing her his etchings was, the Kinsey researchers warned, bound to be disappointed. But lest he take her lack of response personally, the report noted that it was "characteristic of women in general" to be unmoved. In fact, a glimpse of male sex organs might actually inhibit a woman's sexual response.

There were, however, some glaring inconsistencies in the Kinsey portrait of woman as a psychologically unmovable sex object. For one thing, the women studied were *strongly* aroused by movies—not X-rated stag films, but ordinary "commercial" romantic movies. Indeed, they were erotically stimulated more often, and often more intensely, than men were. The Kinsey investigators recognized this as a reaction to the romantic action portrayed, to the portrayal of some particular character or actor in the story; to the "emotional atmosphere" of the movie as a whole, and in some cases, to the woman's feelings about the man with whom she was watching it.

This concept of "romance," rather than graphic portrayals of genital sex, as "women's pornography," has been noted by a number of other prominent researchers. Dr. Robert J. Stoller, the author of *Sex and Gender,* defined pornography as a daydream which induces genital excitement in the observer, chiefly through three essential ingredients: voyeurism, hidden sadism and masochism. But Stoller noted that "women's pornography," which includes true-romance and confession magazines, and probably advice-to-the-lovelorn columns, may deal with seduction, rape, adultery and all sorts of illicit sex. But the *manner* in which such acts are presented is, as Stoller put it, "so subtle as to be completely overlooked by the men who write pornography laws."

Women and young girls in various studies have reported intense genital response—even orgasmic response—to such diverse psychological stimuli as popular song lyrics, television soap operas about illegitimate pregnancy, and most of all, to the rich visual imagery of their own erotic daydreams—sexy pictures, to be sure, but privately screened, and often starring everything *but* the genitals.

In the post-Kinsey generation of sex research, numerous small-scale experiments—conducted mostly by men—have focused on every imaginable aspect of women's and men's responses to pornography. Among the most intriguing:

Whether guilt and anxiety affect women reading erotic stories. (Finding, in a 1969 study of 72 college women at the University of Connecticut: They did feel anxious and guilty—but they also felt aroused.)

Whether husbands and wives respond similarly to erotica. (Finding, in a 1973 study at Purdue University, involving 42 volunteer couples: Yes—and the more "authoritarian" the marriage, the more *both* spouses were sexually aroused by—and also more sternly disapproving of—pornography. "Egalitarian" couples were both less turned on—and less disapproving.)

What kind of erotic films produce the highest degree of female arousal? (Finding, in a study of female undergraduate students at Baylor University: Films showing male-female romantic sex rated highest, followed by mildly erotic group sex, explicit sado-masochism, and lastly, male homosexuality. The women preferred, and were significantly more stimulated by, films in which a man related to a woman, even if cruelly.)

Whether a woman's sexual fantasies and desires increase after seeing porno films and slides. (Finding, in a series of important studies at the University of Hamburg in 1970 and 1972: Yes—both women and men reported increased sexual thoughts and feelings in the 24-hour period after viewing pornographic pictures.)

Whether any mechanical device can measure a woman's immediate genital response to erotic visual stimuli the way male response is tested with before-and-after measurements of penile circumference and acid phosphate levels. (Finding: At the State University of New York at Stony Brook, a vaginal tampon-like probe, equipped with a light and a photocell, was recently developed. This device reportedly can measure increased blood volume in the vagina, revealing objectively whether the wearer is actually experiencing sexual arousal while viewing a sexually explicit film.)

All this elaborate attention has yielded a bewildering mass of new, often conflicting, data about the mechanism of female sexual arousal—but no clear answers as to why, even with newly permissive social attitudes toward woman's sexual activity, she still doesn't appreciate good old-fashioned, genitally focused, man-made porn.

Kinsey didn't take into account the crucial role played by repressive cultural influences in shaping sexual response; the Kinsey report on women took it for granted that whatever was discovered about how women reacted to psychological stimuli was biologically determined. Since Kinsey, however, a number of theorists—again, mostly male—have swung to the opposite extreme, tending to blame inhibiting cultural forces for everything women feel—or don't feel—that differs from men's feelings.

This theory rests on the assumption that the usual male response to the sexual parts of a woman is the norm—though, in fact, it is as much a "conditioned" response as the female's. Some men, to be sure, never find pornography, or any other depersonalized form of sex, as "sexy" as a real relationship with a woman they care about. Some claim to find pinups and X-rated movies boring, and several studies have shown that repeated exposure to porn often causes men to turn off.

Nevertheless, boys in this culture are still taught that the sight of women's breasts, thighs and buttocks are instantly exciting—and a sexy stewardess saying "Fly me" still sells airline tickets to sophisticated men. At the same time, the culture teaches girls that men's bodies are not to be looked at or thought about "that way."

Yet the cultural-conditioning theory is most often advanced only as an explanation for *women's* responses. If women (and girls) were sexually freer, it is suggested, we would turn on as automatically to the sight of—or even the word for—a man's sexual anatomy as men do to ours.

In other words, the assumption here is that women need to be culturally retrained, and that men are the ones to do it. Porn thus becomes a kind of visual teaching aid, representing sex as the ultimate all-American genital-contact sport, complete with rules and code signals. The coach knows enough not to expect his rookie players to warm up the first time out. So the game plan is to give them time—and more training. After all, the theory goes, if you keep telling women it's now O.K. to look, and you keep pushing those pictures at her, and you let her know you *expect* her to turn on, then, by God, she'll make it. She will, in effect, meet the male standard of sexual response. "Instant-on," just like a television set. Unless, of course, she has a problem.

It is certainly true that, despite the lightning speed with which women's sexual preoccupation has moved all the way from frigidity to multiple orgasm, their deeply ingrained negative feelings about genitally focused sex cannot possibly vanish in a one-night stand at the skin flicks.

But the fact is, cultural repression is *not* the whole story, any more than biology was. There is, for instance, substantial evidence concerning the key role played by the male sex hormones (androgens) in the sexuality of both men and women, and of gender-related differences in the erotic arousal process itself. Much of this information comes from the work of Dr. John Money of Johns Hopkins University in Baltimore, author of *Man and Civilization* and co-author, with Dr. Anke Ehrhardt of SUNY, of the more recent *Man & Woman, Boy & Girl*.

Money has suggested that a high level of androgen may influence whether a woman responds erotically to a nude picture of a man. Dr. Frank Beach, a University of California psychologist noted for his investigations of animal sexual behavior, has also theorized that control of the human female's sexual behavior may be primarily hormonal, while the male's is primarily cortical.

But nobody knows for sure. The likeliest explanation is that gender differences—and also individual differences—in erotic response are formed by both *nature* and *nurture,* in varying proportions.

Money and Ehrhardt accept the premise that both men and women can be equally stirred by, say, a nude picture, but they explain that what goes on in the woman's erotic imagination differs fundamentally from what occurs in the man's. This is their description of the difference:

The man sees the girl in the picture as an object of desire. In his imagination, "he takes her out of the picture and has a sexual relationship." He may masturbate, spurred on by his vivid mental picture of her submitting to him.

A woman seeing the same picture may be just as intensely stimulated by it, but in a very different way. Instead of taking the image out of the picture, Money says, she "projects herself into the image" and identifies with the female body on erotic display. Her arousal is then directed toward a particular man toward whom she feels "romantic affection." (Money doesn't theorize on what happens if the woman viewer is a Lesbian or bisexual. I interviewed several bisexual women on this question, and all reported that they see the woman in the picture first as a sexual object and only secondarily as an image to identify with. One bisexual woman I talked to added that when she sees a picture of a man and woman making love, she identifies with the man and imagines herself arousing the woman.)

But what if the picture shows a sexy man? Money's view is that most heterosexual men will pay no attention to it, and that most women won't either—because they cannot identify with or project themselves into the image of the male figure. Thus nobody will find the male nude erotic, except a homosexual male who is attracted to it as a sexual object.

Some recent research in this area, however, casts doubt on Money's belief in the innateness of these responses. Dr. Robert E. Gould, a New York psychiatrist who works with mixed couples' and men's sexual consciousness-raising groups, has found that as men become freer of their conditioned sex roles, *their* responses to the old cues and signals become less "automatic." At present, as Gould and others have observed, most men feel they *must* be aroused by any female body on erotic display, and they must *not* find any male body either erotic or even esthetically appealing.

Audience reactions to male nudity in the theater tend to confirm this view. The manager of one theater showing a nude musical revue *Let My People Come* recently reported that women in the audience are generally much more relaxed and comfortable than the men are—primarily because men are embarrassed to be seen looking at other men's bodies.

Could this be why the male nude photos in *Viva* and *Playgirl* seem so unsexy? It seems likely. If the male editors and photographers do not—or cannot—let themselves see the erotic potential of the male figures they are displaying, the results cannot help but reveal that discomfort.

In a recent interview, Guccione, the publisher of *Penthouse* and *Viva,* described the charged, seductive atmosphere he tries to achieve before shooting pictures of a nude female for *Penthouse.* He claims to spend three days building the model up to a pitch of sexual tension where "you literally have to hold her at bay." It is hard to imagine Guccione talking that way about how to get the sexiest picture of a naked man.

Some women readers have also noted that the male models selected for *Viva* and *Playgirl* often have unusually large penises. This concern with showing men as "well-endowed" is typical of classic male pornography—and represents the notion held by men in general that a large penis equals sexual prowess and potency. Women in general have no such illusion—and no such interest in oversized penises.

This might explain why, though thousands of women saw *Deep Throat,* few remember the name, face or any other distinguishing feature of Harry Reems, the actor who played opposite Linda Lovelace. Unlike the male star of an ordinary romantic movie, Reems failed to give women viewers a character to fall in love with. His "well-endowed" body may have given a tour de force performance—but *he* did not.

The more one examines such evidence, the more one sees that the issue of women's "failure" to respond to porn has less to do with women than with the men who are trying so feverishly to excite them. There is nothing wrong with the female arousal mechanism, but something is clearly wrong with a male pornographer who can't seem to produce a decently sexy picture "for women" to save his box office or magazine. It almost begins to seem as if they don't really *want* to.

In researching this article, I interviewed 50 women—not a scientific sample, but a miscellaneous group, including erotic artists, psychiatrists and sex researchers as well as housewives, college women and a number of writers whose fiction and nonfiction work, like my own, had often focused on women's erotic feelings and responses. This admittedly arbitrary "sample" was as large a group as many, and larger than some, of those studied in the research experiments that make up most of the "medical" literature on women and pornography. Most of my interviewees were in their 30's, a few in their 20's, 40's or 50's, and while they clearly do not represent all women, their views and personal reports did present a strikingly unified picture.

Nearly all of the women I talked to agreed that depersonalized "genitalized" sex, as represented in all classic maleoriented pornography, does not, and probably will never, appeal to them. Most of us did not know a single woman who had been "reached" by the so-called "new porn for women," for the simple reason that, as one woman put it, "it's nothing but porn for men—in drag."

Before speculating on the future—if any—of a genuine women's pornography, I asked each interviewee to name one movie scene, photograph, work of art or literary passage that she personally had found intensely erotic.

The only "classic" pornographic work cited as a "top turn-on" was *Story of O,* by Pauline Réage (generally believed to be a nom de plume for a male author). A deeply masochistic literary fable involving a woman's degradation and willing submission to sexual enslavement, *Story of O,* a best-seller in the nineteen-fifties, was one of the few pornographic novels ever to "reach" an enormous female audience.

One of the women I talked to had written a number of "classic" pornographic novels herself, under a pseudonym. She observed that as erotic writers, women tend to have a more personal, less mechanical approach to the sex scenes than male writers have. A writer and former editor for Olympia Press, the famous French publisher of "quality" erotica, recently observed in *Penthouse:* "What makes sex endlessly fascinating is the human interchange involved, and women seem to know this instinctively." Most male pornography writers are still firmly entrenched in the "Wham, bam, thank you, ma'am" tradition—frequent short sex scenes, with lots of different partners who might all be the same woman in different wigs and costumes. Women, on the other hand, tend to get more into the sexual "subtleties."

Several women in my sample reported being more intensely aroused by paintings or nude sculpture than by books— notably Goya's "Naked Maja," a nude woman clearly offering her body erotically to an unseen man, and Rodin's nude lovers embracing. They also cited Donatello's bronze David, a slender, almost androgynous youth, standing with one foot delicately poised beside the giant severed head of Goliath. The women who found this statue highly erotic explained that it seemed to represent their ideal of male grace—an exquisite, fragile balance between power and almost childlike vulnerability.

One woman said her favorite adolescent fantasy centered on certain Byron poems and letters; she imagined Lord Byron himself making oral love to her while composing them. Another recalled a poignant Genet film that showed two male prisoners reaching hungrily toward each other by kissing and sucking on a straw forced through a chink in the wall between them.

A young novelist described the seminude photograph of a body-building champion in the book *Pumping Iron*. It showed him posed in a darkened theater, flexing his muscles, smiling to himself and wearing only brief trunks and a white fedora, tilted rakishly to catch the light. The appeal of this picture, explained the woman who found it so powerfully erotic, lay "not in the perfect Mr. Universe body, but in the secret grin under the brim of the hat."

To most of the women, a movie scene was the most vividly recalled "turn-on." Most frequently mentioned, in descending order: Clark Gable carrying a struggling Vivien Leigh up the stairs in *Gone with the Wind;* James Mason looming menacingly over Ann Todd in *The Seventh Veil;* the wordless rape scene in *The Fountainhead;* Lesbian sequences in certain pornographic movies such as *The Devil and Miss Jones* and *Flesh Gordon;* Gregory Peck lasciviously observing Jennifer Jones from the rear as she scrubs a floor in *Duel in the Sun;* Marlon Brando's silent rape of Maria Schneider in *Last Tango;* Barbra Streisand reverently—and longingly—touching a sleeping Robert Redford in *The Way We Were.*

A strongly recurrent theme in these reports was romantic masochism—the cold, cruel or indifferent man, and the woman who endures it because she "can't help" loving him. Psychiatrists have said this is rooted, like most "rape fantasies," in a woman's guilt or anxiety feelings about wanting sex. Feminists have added—and some psychiatrists agree— that women will get over these fantasies, once they acquire a positive, assertive self-image. But masochism continues to be a strong component of most women's erotic imagery; sex therapists in my sample confirmed that this is invariably true of their patients.

Next to romantic masochism, the most frequent element in all the erotic highlights mentioned was a mood of tender sensuality, often conveyed through lingering body caresses— whether between a man and woman, two women or even two men. The strong attraction to Lesbian love sequences was often reported by women whose personal "real-life" orientation was totally heterosexual. The psychiatric view of this phenomenon might be that the woman who responds so intensely to a Lesbian love scene probably has strong though latent homosexual feelings. Another view—one advanced by the women themselves—is that what they are responding to is the overpowering tenderness of such scenes—which, unlike many passionate heterosexual love scenes, almost never contain violent or hostile undertones.

In describing and explaining their own erotic responses to movies and art, these women may well have provided all the essential clues about the future of "porn for women."

It may bear a striking resemblance to the kind of total-body sensual focus currently being taught to sexually troubled couples in the sex-therapy clinics, such as those pioneered by Dr. William Masters and Virginia Johnson. This "sensate focus" approach—rather than the old male pattern of zeroing in on the genitals—is what women's erotic response is all about.

If the sex therapists succeed in teaching men that caressing, massaging and nongenital touching can afford intense erotic gratification for both sexes, then perhaps there is hope that everyone—including pornographers—eventually will stop thinking of these movements as mere time-wasting "foreplay" leading up to the main coital bout. Once men are "turned on" to the idea of sex as a bigger picture than a closeup of genitals on the peep-show Movieola (and once women are free enough to *include* the genitals in their fantasy images), we may all get a totally new kind of "human" porn—or better still, no porn at all, because we'll be acting out all our own best erotic fantasies.

Caryl Rivers
THE NEW ANXIETY OF MOTHERHOOD

I stepped into an elevator the other day in the middle of a private conversation. Since I had no choice, I eavesdropped. One young woman was telling another that her therapy group was wrestling with the question of whether or not she should have a baby. She (the prospective mother) was voting yes, her husband was leaning towards no. The rest of the group had not been polled.

Maternity by the Gallup method was a new wrinkle for me. I grew up with the mythology that impending motherhood was an act of God, whose accomplishment was signaled by a wife knitting a pair of booties and wearing a serene smile. I achieved puberty in the fifties, when patriarchy was in flower, Doctor Spock sold briskly, Marilyn Monroe wept after each miscarriage, and penis envy (which drove women to produce babies to compensate for the lack of that marvelous organ) was as much a facet of revealed truth as the existence of The Red Menace.

If you got married, you had kids. It was as simple as that. If you weren't married and got "caught," you had to get married, a fact we sang about in a parody of that old ballad, "Mother."

> M is for the many times you made me,
> O is for the other times you tried.
> T is for the tourist camps we stayed at,
> H is for the hell we raised inside. . . .

That was before the pill and the sexual revolution and the women's movement and Zero Population Growth. The imperative to "Be fruitful and multiply" still holds sway—centuries of tradition do not dematerialize overnight. But an anti-fecundity ethos is building, and where the two currents run into each other, there is, as usual, a great deal of confusion. The woman of childbearing age is tugged in several directions at once. The stress is producing something that might be called The New Anxiety of Motherhood.

"The decision to have a child is more conscious, more momentous, than in the past," says Daniel Callahan, director of the Institute for Society, Ethics and the Life Sciences at Hastings-on-Hudson, N. Y. The institute investigates such questions as ethics and reproductive biology, and Callahan talks to students and to couples who seek genetic counseling. "In the past, everybody just had children. Now they think twice, three times, four times about it. It's odd, young couples seem to think it's the greatest, most complicated choice ever made, even though people have been doing it since the beginning of human history. There's a great deal of self-analysis, a question of whether they will be adequate parents."

The birth rate has been spiraling downward over the past decade to its lowest point in one hundred and fifty years. Is the baby boom in cold storage?

Maybe. But we are in the middle of a recession, and births always dip in hard times. Will prosperity revive the diaper business? Or are we now seeing a true revolution in fertility patterns? The uncertainty is, as Callahan puts it, "driving the demographers crazy."

One expert says that it's possible that people are simply waiting for good times to have children, but he doubts it. Larry L. Bumpass, a University of Wisconsin demographer, says that with the pill and legalized abortion, we will probably see "fertility below replacement." In other words, the population will not explode; rather, it will begin to shrink. As this happens, all the myths and values that have buoyed up the role of motherhood will erode at an accelerated pace. Bumpass says: "Myths that halo even accidental pregnancy may weaken when such an event is no longer seen as inevitable."

The demythification of motherhood is already moving briskly. Here are a few examples:

Motherhood is obsolete: "Large numbers of children are no longer needed to maintain the human species. Woman's sole societal function, so long held in awe and veneration, has become a cursed destructive power."—Feminist Lisa Hobbs.

Motherhood destroys creativity: "If the creative woman has children, she must pay for this indulgence with a long burden of guilt, for her life will be split three ways between them, her husband and her work."—Critic Marya Mannes.

Even happy mothers probably aren't: "Many women have achieved a kind of reconciliation—a conformity—that they interpret as happiness. Since femine happiness is supposed to lie in devoting oneself to husband and children, they do that; *ipso facto,* they assume that they are happy."—Sociologist Jessie Bernard.

Maternal instinct, that old standby, doesn't exist: "There are reflexes, like eye-blinking, and drives, like sex, but there is no innate drive to have children."—William J. Goode, president of the American Sociological Association.

The women's movement, far from being monolithic on the issue, goes off in several directions at once. Some theorists call for a return to worship of the Earth Mother and proclaim that female biology makes women a superior sex. The reign of women, they say, will produce a society that will be nurturing and maternal, as opposed to the violent and destructive mores of men.

Some feminists see childbirth as a revolutionary act. In "Our Bodies, Ourselves," the best-selling handbook produced by the Boston Women's Health Collective, Nancy Hawley writes that her aim in discussing preparation for childbirth is to "reunite women's minds and bodies, not just for the period of childbirth but in an overall program for overcoming our mental and physical oppression as well." She sees bearing a child not as a passive act, but as a conscious decision to join a struggle for the rights of women, "which won't end until we take power, from those who keep the system running, for ourselves. It means a revolution, sister!"

But the main thrust of the movement seems to be away from the woman-as-mother image. Revisionists are busy dismantling the Freudian image of penis envy. They claim that it is a symbol of woman's desire for the economic and social privileges reserved for men. If so, penis envy may go the way of penny loafers and Doris Day movies. The careerist emphasis of the movement is strong: better a title on the door than a baby crawling on the floor.

For a woman of childbearing age, it isn't easy to sort this all out. Is she really an Earth Mother whose biological powers can transform the planet? Is she copping out of the movement if she goes to a split-level in Scarsdale instead of to law school? Is having a baby a revolutionary act or the selfish indulgence of a planet-polluter? Can she be a decent mother and still have a profession? Will a baby spoil her relationship with a man? Should she try for a "fun marriage" instead? Or not marry at all? When I was in college, a glittery diamond on the third finger, left hand, meant an end to choosing. One could accept the inevitable, with a grateful sigh. White gown, first apartment, baby bottles, were sure to follow. For young women today, the choices are dizzying:

Have sex, or don't. Have it with a man, or a woman. Use the pill, the IUD, the diaphragm. Have an abortion. Marry, or don't. Do have children. Don't have children. Have a career. Have a career and a child. Have a husband, but no child. Have a child, but no husband.

It is not surprising that the anxiety quotient among young women is on the rise. It is particularly acute for women in their late twenties or early thirties who are making headway in a profession. They have the sense they are skating close to a biological precipice.

"It's the only real deadline you've got," says one woman who has a promising job in city government. At 27, she is aware that by her family's timetable, she is already late. Her great-grandmother and her grandmother were pregnant by the time they were 18. Her mother held off until 26. Like many women, she feels the pressure from opposite currents. She is dedicated to her job and works long hours. At the same time, she is suspicious of the heavy emphasis on careers that is now chic in the movement.

"A lot of values can get lost—values that were traditionally in the care of women," she says.

That idea has been in her mind of late, because she has been involved in a project with senior citizens who make tapestries, a sharp contrast to the work-fifteen-hours-a-day, get-it-done-yesterday, move-up-the-ladder pace of politics.

"The idea that life involves a healthy amount of time doing other things can get lost around here," she says, nodding toward the other offices along the corridor of a skyscraper.

She has a sense, as do so many other women, of the Byzantine intricacies of juggling a career and a baby. She has a stable relationship with a man, but finds it hard to reconcile the demands of her job with the pressures of motherhood. She is not yet sure enough of her strengths to come to a decision. She is not closing any doors, and she has time—but the clock is ticking.

Another young woman in her early thirties has taken a hard look at the women in her family. They are possessive matriarchs, and that frightens her. She doesn't say so, but one can sense she sees a prophecy there; and if so, she wants to run like hell in the other direction. So many young women have seen their mothers' lives go empty and vacant, watched them turn into compulsive shoppers who fill extra closets with clothes they do not need; or into clutching mamas who cannot turn their children loose; or into wives who go about their chores with their faces rigid with resentment toward the man whose life is linked with theirs because of the children. I have heard many women talk lately of mothers sliding toward breakdown, of irrational screaming and fits of depression. They seem puzzled, these women. They have done all that was expected of them, whatever it cost, so why is their universe falling suddenly, terribly apart?

Some young women have put an end to the questioning. They have turned off the clock. They have decided not to have children.

"I see a lot of people who are making an active, conscious decision not to have children," says Dr. Carol Nadelson, a psychiatrist on the staff of Boston's Beth Israel Hospital. "Sometimes it is a very reasonable decision. But sometimes I hear people say, 'Children have to have all these things, and I don't think I can provide them.' They're saying, 'I *can't* do it,' not 'I don't want to.'"

The note of anxiety is sounded in the words of some who

have chosen to be "non-parents." A Georgia woman says, "I would be a very nervous parent and probably overprotective. If the child was a girl she would have to be a Girl Scout and get good grades or I would never understand her." A woman in New Jersey says her unhappy childhood was a large factor in her decision. A student in Boston says he has little patience with children and probably wouldn't be a good father.

Non-parents have a movement of their own now, called NON—the National Organization for Non-parents. Ellen Peck, one of its founders, wrote a book called *The Baby Trap* a few years back and was flooded with mail from people without children who said they were tired of being viewed as selfish monsters or anti-social freaks.

Peck is an unlikely-looking crusader against Motherhood. She has been described in print as a Renaissance madonna and a cheerleader. Such descriptions may gall her, but she is stuck with a first-to-be-pinned-in-junior-year face. She works out of her apartment in Baltimore, and she is an articulate young woman, *sotto voce;* no fanatical glint in the eye or tremor in the voice. She says she is not anti-child or anti-Mom, but she wants to see a day when a childfree (she does not say child*less*)lifestyle is considered a reasonable option for couples.

NON has gathered an impressive array of statistics to back up its motto: None Is Fun. For example, when Dr. Harold Feldman, a Cornell University sociologist, did a study of 850 married couples, he concluded: "Those couples with children had a significantly lower level of marital satisfaction than did those without children." NON produces census figures to show that 1 out of 25 wives between 18 and 25 now expects to have no children. In 1967, the ratio was 1 out of every 100.

The number of couples opting for a childfree lifestyle seems to be small but growing. Back in the days of "togetherness" anybody who said he or she didn't want kids was considered a pervert or a freak. No longer. In a casual conversation in a university corridor recently, three students were discussing the question. One girl said she wanted kids; a second wasn't sure; and the third, a senior, said he and his fiancée had already decided not to have children. Both were going into broadcasting, a highly mobile, competitive profession. They felt no censure from their peers, but the parents were another story. His fincée's mother had come around, reluctantly. She had talked about the custom of saving the top layer of the wedding cake to eat at the birth of the first child. "But I guess it would rot before you ate it," she sighed.

NON has launched a frontal attack on the motherhood myth (NON calls it pronatalism) that lurks everywhere: in the dolls that little girls are given to cuddle, the school books in which all women are "Mom." Of certain TV ads—"There's nothing like the face of a kid eating a Hershey bar"—Ellen Peck says, "There's nothing like the face of a kid having a tantrum."

Although Peck sees the goals of NON and the women's movement as complementary, one California woman wrote in to cancel her membership because she found NON anti-feminist. NON, she said, simply shifted the emphasis from woman as child-centered to woman as husband-centered. "There is rarely any emphasis placed on women achieving identity through their own self-actualization, rather than through a man."

It seems a legitimate complaint. The material that NON distributes leans heavily on the discomforts of having kids. In one cartoon, a well-dressed couple sits on a couch, surrounded by a pack of devilishly grinning children who are taking apart the furniture, belting each other and writing on the walls. A grotesquely pregnant mother smiles at the couple and says, "And when are you two going to have kids?"

Non-parenthood, on the other hand, is presented as cycling side by side, dinners by candlelight and making love in Martinique. One wonders if this is any less romanticized than the "Brady Bunch" image of adorable kids and beautiful Mommy? Non-parenthood may have its mythology too.

If "pronatalism" has its roots coiled deep in social custom, anti-natalism is starting to make inroads. NON is getting good press; Zero Population Growth has made "Stop at Two" a familiar slogan. Even the women's magazines with the most aggressive tradition of hearth and home are starting to write about non-parenthood. Add to this the dropping birth rate and the careerist emphasis of mainstream feminism, and it all can make one particular citizen very nervous: the pregnant woman.

"She's a sidshow freak. How many pregnant women do you see on the streets?" says Maureen Finnerty Turner, the director of an organization called COPE (Coping with the Overall Pregnancy Experience).

"All the movements—ZPG, abortion reform, non-parenthood—they've taken their toll. The pregnant woman is a liability."

Ms. Turner says that one of the women in the group was approached on the street by a stranger who said, "Don't you know you're polluting the earth with another baby?"

One of the first questions pregnant women are asked, according to Ms. Turner, is: "Are you going to keep it?" She adds, "It's OK on the first pregnancy, more hassle on the second, and God help you on your third.

"I've heard women complain that their doctors—men who sympathize with the feminist movement—look at them when they come in with a second or third pregnancy and say, 'Of course you're going to have an abortion.' I've been a feminist for years, but when I had my second child, people said, 'Ah ha, Maureen, you've been caught!' It was a planned pregnancy. I should have said, 'It's my uterus and I'll do what I want with it!'"

COPE operates out of the first floor of Maureen's home in Boston's South End. The quarters are crowded. Tiny overalls are draped across a high chair and cans of Gerber's strained carrots sit on top of a filing cabinet. COPE sponsors support groups for pregnant women, mothers of toddlers, and women who have had abortions. It has no funding other than minimal membership fees. The volunteer staff tries to wrestle with paperwork and roaming toddlers at the same time.

COPE is one of the few organizations in the country geared to helping the pregnant woman. A three-line mention in a national women's magazine brought in a barrage of 300 letters from 40 states. But COPE can barely keep up with its burgeoning local membership. It is seeking foundation money, but its members fear that to the dispensers of money—

as well as to the world at large—the pregnant woman is a curious and not very important phenomenon.

Turner, a psychiatric nurse and therapist, realized during her first pregnancy that the pregnant woman is isolated; she's the victim of confusing social myths, and in a mobile society she's shorn of the traditional support of the extended family. The dropping birth rate means that she's not going to meet many other pregnant women in the course of her normal social activities. While there have been significant advances in the medical technology of childbirth, much less attention is paid to the psychological experience.

In the COPE office, feeding and cuddling their year-old sons, two members of COPE talked about that experience.

"A massive chemical change takes place," says Nancy Fries Harmon, an intense, articulate young woman with short-cropped hair. "It was like being on a hallucinogen and trying to exist in a straight world. Nobody took me seriously. My perceptions were different. I was the only pregnant person I knew. I was seven months pregnant when I joined COPE. When I realized that the things I was feeling were common to other pregnant women, I was angry enough to want to work to help other women. The world isn't geared to the problems of pregnant women, or women with children."

Karen Hutchinson, an unmarried mother who chose the role of single parent, was fighting the exhaustion of a bad cold and trying to cope with the incessant demands of a one-year-old.

"Adjusting to the idea of having a child made it a whole new world for me," she says. "The old ways of relating to the world just didn't make sense any more."

"You are all alone with these changes," Nancy says. "New mothers tend to relive old life crises. You think maybe you're going mad."

Isolated from other pregnant women, separated from parents by lifestyle if not by geography, the pregnant woman can develop the paranoid feelings of an oppressed minority. No one seems to care.

Nancy, who was separated from her husband after the birth of her son, says: "Some of my men friends think my attitude (about the importance of COPE) is 'cute,' but not very important. To me it's deadly important."

"People don't think pregnant women and new mothers need help," says Karen. "They say: 'But you're just doing what you're supposed to do.'"

When a pregnancy is planned, Maureen Turner says, a woman is given no licence to complain of problems or ask for help. "'You made your bed, now lie in it—that's the attitude."

Nancy says, "It finally dawned on me that women were the ones who had to do something. We had to take our own needs seriously enough."

All three are concerned because society seems to be putting less value these days on the nurturing role. "Nobody's making it known in 1974 that producing and raising children is important work," claims Ms. Turner.

Nancy adds: "Women themselves have started saying that working in the home isn't valuable. I got so concerned with my own liberation that I thought the only solution for me was to go out and get a job after I brought the baby home. I didn't think I should want to be home with my child. But I've chosen motherhood, and I've had to defend my choice. I value it above everything else, but it isn't all of my life. I have to find a way of mothering that isn't all-consuming. A lot of us watched our mothers be nothing but mothers—and then go through a menopause crisis because there wasn't anyone to mother any more."

Listening to women talk of new ways of mothering, of parenthood as just one option, of non-parenthood and of childbirth as revolution, it is easy to get the impression that everything is changing, that none of those quaint old customs, like getting pregnant to trap a man, exist any more. But there are places—a lot of places—where the nineteen-fifties I grew up in just never left. Dr. Joy Browne, a psychologist who works in a clinic in a middle-class suburb, sees the young matrons who say, "My husband isn't interested in me any more. I'm losing him. I'll have a baby." There are the girls who want to marry their boyfriends, so they stop taking the pill; and the women who see the youngest child go off to school and think, "I can't do anything in the real world," and get pregnant again because they know that's something they *can* do. There are women who get pregnant just because their lives are, as Joy Browne puts it, "icky, muddy, desperate."

Scariest of all are the teenagers. They take chances, not believing it will happen. They are vague about the details of contraception. When it does happen, they think that having a baby will be like having a Barbie doll to play with.

They want to keep their babies, even when their mothers drag them into abortion clinics. Joy Browne calls it "the goddamned Vanessa Redgrave syndrome."

They say, "Times have changed, my mother doesn't understand!" They have no idea that it is a different thing for a 15-year-old girl with no visible means of support to have a love child than it is for a rich and famous movie star. They are still children themselves. I asked a group of pregnant 13- and 14-year-olds what they thought they would be doing ten years from now. They stared at me; quite clearly, no such thought had ever entered their minds. They lived in a child's world where the future meant only the next day.

I was thinking of them when I read the following fact: There is only one segment of the population in which the birth rate is going up, not down—the teenagers.

But for the girls who make it out of high school without getting pregnant, particularly for those who go on to college, or live in middle-class urban areas, choice is becoming a fact of life. Anxiety is one of its penalties—the price of freedom, one might say. It seems, to me at least, that the idea of parenthood as a conscious choice, part of a life plan, is immensely preferable to an inevitable happening one can neither avoid nor control. The lives of too many women have been blighted by passivity and the sense that they were perpetual victims. The choice not to be a parent should be honored. One can live a rich, full life without progeny.

But I get a little anxious myself when I hear people talk of making childbirth a specialized occupation for the very few, rather like plumbing. I am suspicious of utopian plans to replace the family unit. We ought to remember that the relation between parent and child is a knot coiled of vein and sinew, made of the strongest tissue we know. If our families can tear us apart, they can also bind our wounds, draw in around us like a cave to keep out the uncaring, rocketing world. Artificial substitutes often flounder; the communes set up by the young drift apart in the currents of a mobile society. The real family spreads and floats, but when there is trouble, knots up again. It has a biological imperative to do so.

"Home is the place where, when you have to go there, they have to take you in."—Robert Frost.

Mary Daly
GOD IS A VERB

My first feminist book, *The Church and the Second Sex,* was published in 1968, before the cresting of the second wave of feminism. The writing began in 1965 in a small medieval city, Fribourg, Switzerland, where I lived for seven years. It was completed in 1967 in Boston. It was written with a great sense of pride, anger, and hope.

In 1971, after a brief, turbulent history, *The Church and the Second Sex* went out of print. It formally died. I tried to "reason" with the publisher that there was a demand for it, pointing out that I had received many letters and telephone calls, especially from women taking or teaching feminist studies, asking why the book wasn't available. But reason, as I had always understood the term, had no effect upon the publishing house patriarchs, who refused to move. So I moved on to other things, including a dramatic/traumatic change of consciousness from "radical Catholic" to postchristian feminist. My graduation from the Catholic church was formalized by a self-conferred diploma, my second feminist book, *Beyond God the Father: Toward a Philosophy of Women's Liberation,* which appeared in 1973. The journey in time/space that took place between the publication dates of the two books could not be described adequately by terrestrial calendars and maps. Experientially, it was hardly even a mere trip to the moon, but more like leapfrogging galaxies in a mind voyage to further and further stars. Several woman-light years had separated me from *The Church and the Second Sex,* whose author I sometimes have trouble recalling.

Then, in 1974, with the imponderable logic that characterizes the Divinities of the Publishing World, the book's publishers informed me of their celestial desire that it appear on earth once again. Oh Goddess: a Second Coming? Startled, I contemplated this new revelation. The Divine Word had been spoken. Now, what response should I give about this strange book and its strange author who had inhabited a distant world? There was of course the biblical answer: "Let it be done according to Thy Word." However, to a postchristian feminist, that hardly seemed an appropriate response. Therefore, I would have to devise some unique solution to the subtle and intriguing problem posed by these Godfathers. What were the possibilities? An updated, revised edition, perhaps? I went to my bookcase and took the book off the shelf. Opening it with a sense of reluctance, I felt as if this were the journal of a half-forgotten foremother, whose quaintness should be understood in historical context and treated with appropriate respect.

Opening the book at random, I found myself in Chapter Seven, "Toward Partnership: Some Modest Proposals." I read a few pages and discovered that the author was proposing that there be equality between men and women in the Church (sic, with capital "C"). Why, I wondered, would anyone want "equality" in the church? In a statement that I had given to the press only three or four woman-light years distant from now, I had explained that a woman's asking for equality in the church would be comparable to a black person's demanding equality in the Klu Klux Klan. How could the author of this book have been so obtuse . . .? But then, the publication date was 1968 A.D. Flipping through a few pages, I noted that the author had used the rather pompous editorial "we" instead of "I," and had written "they" to refer to women, instead of "we." Why did she say "we" when she meant "I," and "they" when she meant "we"? I noted with a sense of embarrassment for her that she used the term "man" as if it were a generic term. I perceived that she had hoped to reform Christianity. Clearly, it would be impossible to "revise" this book in the year 1975 of feminist postchristian time/space (hereafter referred to as A.F. or *Anno Feminarum*).

What to do? Since the Christian model of resignation to the will of the Proprietor of the Word is dysfunctional in the year 1975 A.F., I considered simply refusing to allow this Second Coming of *The Church and the Second Sex*. However, I hesitated at the prospect of such a drastic refusal, partly because women continued to ask for the book. Then another possibility occurred to me: let it become incarnate again, with a new postchristian introduction by myself. The advantages of this last option became apparent, the longer I reflected upon the dilemma posed by time warp. First, since the book is a carefully researched historical record, and since the material it contains is difficult to obtain anywhere else, this Second Coming would make the data available again for those engaged in feminist studies. Second, the book itself is now part of women's history, and as such it is revealing. It represents a stage of thought, feelings, hope, politics that can now be reflected upon from the perspective of new feminist time/space. Since I was, in an earlier incarnation, the author of that book, I am in a unique position to bring it forth again in a new light, to tell its story and then, in the new introduction, to become its critic and reviewer. And so it was the Morning of the Second Daly. I saw that it was a good idea. . . .

As a result of the First Coming of *The Church and the Second Sex* . . . I "lectured" to academic audiences and women's groups across the country about the sexism of the Christian tradition. Often in the late sixties I encountered hostility in women, not toward the partriarchs whose misogynism I exposed, but toward me for exposing them.

By about 1970 this phenomenon of misplaced anger had almost disappeared. More and more people had caught up with the First Daly, and the lines that formerly had elicited hostility brought forth cheers. But the ''I'' who was then standing before the friendly audiences and tossing out the familiar phrases was already disconnected from the words, already moving through a new time/space. I often heard the old words as though a stranger were speaking them—some personage visiting from the past. My concern was no longer limited to "equality" in the church or anywhere else. I did not really care about unimaginative reform but instead began dreaming new dreams of a women's revolution. This was becoming a credible dream, because a community of sisterhood was coming into being, into be-ing. In the hearing/

healing presence of my sisters I had grown ready to try writing/ speaking New Words.

The breakthrough to New Words found expression in *Beyond God the Father: Toward a Philosophy of Women's Liberation,* which is excerpted here. In the introduction to that book I explained: "To exist humanly is to name the self, the world, and God. The evolving spiritual consciousness of women is nothing less than this beginning to speak humanly—a reclaiming of the right to name. The liberation of language is rooted in the liberation of ourselves.

"It would be a mistake to imagine that the new speech of women can be equated simply with women speaking men's words. What is happening is that women are really *hearing ourselves* and each other, and out of this supportive hearing emerge *new words.*"

The biblical and popular image of God as a great patriarch in heaven, rewarding and punishing according to his mysterious and seemingly arbitrary will, has dominated the imagination of millions over thousands of years. The symbol of the Father God, spawned in the human imagination and sustained as plausible by patriarchy, has in turn rendered service to this type of society by making its mechanisms for the oppression of women appear right and fitting. If God in "his" heaven is a father ruling "his" people, then it is in the "nature" of things and according to divine plan and the order of the universe that society be male-dominated. Within this context a mystification of roles takes place: the husband dominating his wife represents God "himself." . . .

As the Women's Movement begins to have its effect upon the fabric of society, transforming it from patriarchy into something that never existed before, into a diarchal situation that is radically new, it can become the greatest single challenge to the major religions of the world, Western and Eastern—all of which are essentially sexist. Beliefs and values that have held sway for thousands of years will be questioned as never before. This revolution may well be also the greatest single hope for survival of spiritual consciousness on this planet.

There are some who persist in claiming that the liberation of women will only mean that new characters will assume the same old roles, and that nothing will change essentially in structures, ideologies, and values. This supposition is often based on the observation that the very few women in "masculine" occupations often behave much as men do. This kind of reasoning is not at all to the point, for it fails to take into account the fact that tokenism does not change stereotypes or social systems but works to preserve them, since it dulls the revolutionary impulse. The minute proportion of women in the United States who occupy such roles (such as congresswomen, judges, business executives, doctors, and so on) have been trained by men in institutions defined and designed by men, and they have been pressured subtly to operate according to male rules. There are no alternate models. . . .

What *is* to the point is an emergence of woman-consciousness such as has never before taken place. It is unimaginative and out of touch with what is happening in the Women's Movement to assume that the becoming of women will simply mean uncritical acceptance of structures, beliefs, symbols, norms, and patterns of behavior that have been given priority by society under male domination. Rather, this becoming will act as a catalyst for radical change in our culture. . . . What *can* effect basic alteration in the system is a potent influence *from without*. Women who reject patriarchy have this power and indeed *are* this power of transformation that is ultimately threatening to things as they are.

The roles and structures of patriarchy have been developed and sustained in accordance with an artificial polarization of human qualities into the traditional sexual stereotypes. The image of the person in authority and the accepted understanding of "his" role has corresponded to the eternal masculine stereotype, which implies hyper-rationality (in reality, frequently reducible to pseudo-rationality), "objectivity," aggressivity, the possession of dominating and manipulative attitudes toward persons and the environment, and the tendency to construct boundaries between the self (and those identified with the self) and "the Other." The caricature of human being which is represented by this stereotype depends for its existence upon the opposite caricature—the eternal feminine. This implies hyper-emotionalism, passivity, self-abnegation, and so on.

By becoming whole persons women can generate a counterforce to the stereotype of the leader, challenging the artificial polarization of human characteristics into sex-role identification. There is no reason to assume that women who have the support of each other to criticize not only the feminine stereotype but the masculine stereotype as well will simply adopt the latter as a model for ourselves. On the contrary, what is happening is that women are developing a wider range of qualities and skills. This is beginning to encourage and in fact demand a comparably liberating process in men— a phenomenon which has begun in men's liberation groups and which is taking place every day within the context of personal relationships. The becoming of androgynous human persons implies a radical change in the fabric of human consciousness and in styles of human behavior.

This change is already threatening the credibility of the religious symbols of our culture. Since many of these have been used to justify oppression, such a challenge should be seen as redemptive. Religious symbols fade and die when the cultural situation that gave rise to them and supported them ceases to give them plausibility. Such an event generates anxiety, but it is part of the risk involved in a faith which accepts the relativity of all symbols and recognizes that clinging to these as fixed and ultimate is self-destructive and idolatrous. . . .

The various theologies that . . . in one way or another objectify "God" as a *being*, thereby attempt in a self-contradictory way to envisage transcendent reality as finite. "God" then functions to legitimate the existing social, economic, and political status quo, in which women and other victimized groups are subordinate.

"God" can be used oppressively against women in a number of ways. First, it occurs in an overt manner when theologians proclaim women's subordination to be God's will. . . .

Second, even in the absence of such explicitly oppressive justification, the phenomenon is present when one-sex symbolism for God and for the human relationship to God is used. The following passage from Gregory Baum's *Man Becoming* illustrates the point:

To believe that God is Father is to become aware of oneself not as a stranger, not as an outsider or an alienated person, but as a son who belongs or a person appointed to a marvelous destiny, which he shares with the whole community. To believe that God is Father means to be able to say "we" in regard to all men.

A woman whose consciousness has been aroused can say that such language makes her aware of herself as a stranger, as an outsider, as an alienated person, not as a daughter who belongs or who is appointed to a marvelous destiny. She cannot belong to *this* without assenting to her own lobotomy.

Third, even when the basic assumptions of God-language appear to be nonsexist, and when language is somewhat purified of fixation upon maleness, it is damaging and implicitly compatible with sexism if it encourages detachment from the reality of the human struggle against oppression in its concrete manifestations. . . .

The new insight of women is bringing us to a point beyond such direct and indirect theological oppressiveness that traditionally has centered around discussions of "God." It is becoming clear that if God-language is even implicitly compatible with oppressiveness, failing to make clear the relation between intellection and liberation, then it will either have to be developed in such a way that it becomes explicitly relevant to the problem of sexism or else dismissed. . . . In my thinking, the specific criterion which implies a mandate to reject certain forms of God-talk is expressed in the question: Does this language hinder human becoming by reinforcing sex-role socialization? Expressed positively—the question is: Does it *encourage* human becoming toward psychological and social fulfillment, toward an androgynous mode of living, toward transcendence? . . .

Mary Daly

Many questions that are of burning importance to women now simply have not occurred in the past (and to a large extent in the present) to those with "credentials" to do theology. Other questions may have been voiced timidly but quickly squelched as stupid, irrelevant, or naïve. Therefore, attempts by women theologians now merely to "update" or to reform theology within acceptable patterns of question-asking are not likely to get very far.

Moreover, within the context of the prevailing social climate it has been possible for scholars to be aware of the most crudely dehumanizing texts concerning women in the writings of religious "authorities" and theologians—from Augustine to Aquinas, to Luther, to Knox, to Barth—and at the same time to treat their unverified opinions on far more imponderable matters with utmost reverence and respect. That is, the blatant misogynism of these men has not been the occasion of a serious credibility gap even for those who have disagreed on this "point." It has simply been ignored or dismissed as trivial. By contrast, in the emerging consciousness of women this context is beginning to be perceived in its full significance and as deeply relevant to the world view in which such "authorities" have seen other seemingly unrelated subjects, such as the problem of God. Hence the present awakening of the hitherto powerless sex demands an explosion of creative imagination that can withstand the disapproval of orthodoxy and overreach the boundaries cherished by conventional minds.

The driving revelatory force that is making it possible for women to speak—and to *hear* each other speak—more authentically about God is courage in the face of the risks that attend the liberation process. Since the projections of patriarchal religion have been blocking the dynamics of existential courage by offering the false security of alienation, that is, of self-reduction in sex roles, there is reason to hope for the emergence of a new religious consciousness in the confrontation with sexism that is now in its initial stages. The becoming of women may be not only the doorway to deliverance which secular humanism has passionately fought for—but also a doorway *to* something, that is, a new phase in the human spirit's quest for God.

This becoming who we really are requires existential courage to confront the experience of nothingness. All human beings are threatened by nonbeing. . . . I am suggesting that at this point in history women are in a unique sense called to be the bearers of existential courage in society.

People attempt to overcome the threat of nonbeing by denying the self. The outcome of this is ironic: that which is dreaded triumphs, for we are caught in the self-contradictory bind of shrinking our being to avoid nonbeing. The only alternative is self-actualization in spite of the ever-present nothingness. Part of the problem is that people, women in particular, who are seemingly incapable of a high degree of self-actualization have been made such by societal structures that are products of human attempts to create security. Those who are alienated from their own deepest identity do receive a kind of security in return for accepting very limited and undifferentiated identities. The woman who single-mindedly accepts the role of "housewife," for example, may to some extent avoid the experience of nothingness but she also avoids a fuller participation in being, which would be her only real security and source of community. Submerged in such a role, she cannot achieve a breakthrough to creativity. Many strong women are worn out in the struggle to break out of these limits before reaching the higher levels of intellectual discovery or of creativity.

The beginning of a breakthrough means a realization that there is an existential conflict between the self and structures that have given such crippling security. This requires confronting the shock of nonbeing with the courage to be. It means facing the nameless anxieties of fate, which become concretized in loss of jobs, friends, social approval, health, and even life itself. Also involved is anxiety of guilt over refusing to do what society demands, a guilt which can hold one in its grip long after it has been recognized as false. Finally, there is the anxiety of meaninglessness, which can be overwhelming at times when the old simple meanings, role definitions, and life expectations have been rooted out and rejected openly and one emerges into a world without models.

This confrontation with the anxiety of nonbeing is revelatory, making possible the relativization of structures that are seen as human products, and therefore not absolute and ultimate. It drives consciousness beyond fixation upon "things as they are." Courage to be is the key to the revelatory power of the feminist revolution.

With the rise of feminism, women have come to see the necessity of conflict, of letting rage surface and of calling forth a will to liberation. Yet, partially because there is such an essential contrast between feminism and patriarchal religion's destructive symbols and values, and partially because women's lives are intricately bound up with those of men— biologically, emotionally, socially, and professionally—it is clear that Women's Liberation is essentially linked with full human liberation.

Women generally can see very well that the Movement will self-destruct if we settle for vengeance. The more imminent danger, then, is that some women will seek premature reconciliation, not allowing themselves to see the depth and implications of feminism's essential opposition to sexist society. It can be easy to leap on the bandwagon of "human liberation" without paying the price in terms of polarization, tensions, risk, and pain that the ultimate objective of real human liberation demands. . . .

It might seem that the women's revolution should just go about its business of generating a new consciousness, without worrying about God. I suggest that the fallacy involved in this would be an overlooking of a basic question that is implied in human existence and that the pitfall in such an oversight is cutting off the radical potential of the Movement itself.

It is reasonable to take the position that sustained effort toward self-transcendence requires keeping alive in one's consciousness the question of ultimate transcendence, that is, of God. It implies recognition of the fact that we have no power *over* the ultimately real, and that whatever authentic power we have is derived from *participation* in ultimate reality. This awareness, always hard to sustain, makes it possible to be free of idolatry even in regard to one's own cause, since it tells us that all presently envisaged goals, lifestyles, symbols, and societal structures may be transitory. This is the meaning that the question of God should have for liberation, sustaining a concern that is really open to the future, in other words, that is really ultimate. Such a concern will not become fixated upon limited objectives.

Feminists in the past have in a way been idolatrous about such objectives as the right to vote. Indeed, this right is due to women in justice and it is entirely understandable that feminists' energies were drained by the efforts needed to achieve even such a modicum of justice. But from the experience of such struggles we are in a position now to distrust token victories within a societal and structural framework that renders them almost meaningless. The new wave of feminism desperately needs to be not only many-faceted but cosmic and ultimately religious in its vision. This means reaching outward and inward toward the God beyond and beneath the gods who have stolen our identity.

The idea that human beings are "to the image of God" is an intuition whose implications could hardly be worked through under patriarchal conditions. If it is true that human beings have projected "God" in their own image, it is also true that we can evolve beyond the projections of earlier stages of consciousness. It is the creative potential itself in human beings that is the image of God. As the essential victims of the archaic God-projections, women can bring this process of creativity into a new phase. This involves iconoclasm—the breaking of idols. Even—and perhaps especially—through the activity of its most militantly atheistic and a-religious members, the Movement is smashing images that obstruct the becoming of the image of God. The basic idol-breaking will be done on the level of internalized images of male superiority, on the plane of exorcising them from consciousness and from the cultural institutions that breed them. . . .

One of the false deities to be dethroned is the God of explanation, or "God as a stopgap for the incompleteness of our knowledge," as Dietrich Bonhoeffer called "him." This serves sometimes as the legitimation of . . . such anomic [purposeless] occurrences as the suffering of a child. Such phenomena are "explained" as being God's will. So also are socially prevailing inequalities of power and privilege, by a justifying process which easily encourages masochistic attitudes. Clearly, this deity does not encourage commitment to the task of analyzing and eradicating the social, economic, and psychological roots of suffering. As marginal beings who are coming into awareness, women are in a situation to see that "God's plan" is often a front for men's plans and a cover for inadequacy, ignorance, and evil. Our vantage point offers opportunities for dislodging this deity from its revered position on the scale of human delusions.

Another idol is the God of otherworldliness. The most obvious face of this deity in the past has been that of the Judge whose chief activity consists in rewarding and punishing after death. As Simone de Beauvoir indicated, women have been the major consumers of this religious product. Since there has been so little self-realization possible by the female sex "in this life," it was natural to focus attention on the next. As mass consumers of this image, women have the power to remove it from the market, mainly by living full lives here and now. I do not mean to advocate a mere re-utterance of the "secularization" theology that was so popular in the sixties. . . . If women can sustain the courage essential to liberation, this can give rise to a deeper "otherworldliness"—an awareness that the process of creating a counterworld to the counterfeit "this world" presented to consciousness by the societal structures that oppress us *is* participation in eternal life. . . .

A third idol, intimately related to those described above, is the God who is the Judge of "sin," who confirms the rightness of the rules and roles of the reigning system, maintaining false consciences and self-destructive guilt feelings. Women have suffered both mentally and physically from this deity, in whose name we have been informed that birth control and abortion are unequivocally wrong, that we should be subordinate to husbands, that we must be present at rituals and services in which men have all the leadership roles and in which we are degraded not only by enforced passivity but also verbally and symbolically. Although this is most blatant in the arch-conservative religions, the God who imposes false guilt is hardly absent from liberal Protestantism and Judaism, where his presence is more subtle. Women's growth in self-respect will deal the deathblow to this as well as to the other demons dressed as Gods.

I have indicated that because the becoming of women involves a radical encounter with nothingness, it bears with it a new surge of ontological [concerning the nature and relations of being] hope. This hope is essentially active. The passive hope that has been so prevalent in the history of religious attitudes corresponds to the objectified God from whom one may anticipate favors. Within that frame of reference, human beings have tried to relate to ultimate reality as an object to be known, cajoled, manipulated. The tables are turned, however, for the objectified "God" has a way of reducing "his" producers to objects who lack capacity for autonomous action. In contrast to this, the God who is power of being acts as a moral power summoning women and men to act out of our deepest hope and to become who we can be. . . .

This hope is communal rather than merely individualistic, because it is grounded in the two-edged courage to be. That is, it is hope coming from the experience of individuation *and* participation. It drives beyond the objectified God that is imagined as limited in benevolence, bestowing blessing upon "his" favorites. The power of being is that in which all finite beings participate, but not on a "one-to-one" basis, since this power is in all, while transcending all. Communal hope involves in some manner a profound interrelationship with other finite beings, human and nonhuman. Ontological communal hope, then, is cosmic. Its essential dynamic is directed to the universal community.

Finally, ontological hope is revolutionary. Since the insight in which it is grounded is the double-edged intuition of nonbeing and of being, it extends beyond the superstitious fixations of technical reason. The latter when it is cut off from the intuitive knowledge of ontological reason cannot get beyond superstition. The rising consciousness that women are experiencing of our dehumanized situation has the power to turn attention around from the projections of our culture to the radically threatened human condition. Insofar as women are true to this consciousness, we have to be the most radical of revolutionaries, since the superstition revealed to us is omnipresent and plagues even the other major revolutionary movements of our time. Knowing that a black or white, Marxist or Capitalist, countercultural or bourgeois male chauvinist deity (human or divine) will not differ essentially from his opposite, women will be forced in a dramatic way to confront the most haunting of human questions, the question of God. This confrontation may not find its major locus within the theological academy or the institutional churches and it may not always express itself in recognizable theological or philosophical language. However, there is a dynamism in the ontological affirmation of self that reaches out toward the nameless God. In hearing and naming ourselves out of the depths, women are naming *toward* God, which is what theology always should have been about. Unfortunately, it tended to stop at fixing names *upon* God, which deafened us to our own potential for self-naming.

It has sometimes been argued that anthropomorphic symbols for "God" are important and even necessary because the fundamental powers of the cosmos otherwise are seen as impersonal. One of the insights characteristic of the rising woman-consciousness is that this kind of dichotomizing between cosmic power and the personal need not be. That is, it is not necessary to anthropomorphize or to reify transcendence in order to relate to this personally. In fact, the process is demonic in some of its consequences. The dichotomizing-reifying-projecting syndrome has been characteristic of patriarchal consciousness, making "the Other" the repository of the contents of the lost self. Since women are now beginning to recognize in ourselves the victims of such dichotomizing processes, the insight extends to other manifestations of the pathological splitting-off of reality into falsely conceived opposites.

Why indeed must "God" be a noun? Why not a verb—the most active and dynamic of all? Hasn't the naming of "God" as a noun been an act of murdering that dynamic Verb? And isn't the Verb infinitely more personal than a mere static noun? The anthropomorphic symbols for God may be intended to convey personality, but they fail to convey that God is Be-ing. Women now who are experiencing the shock of nonbeing and the surge of self-affirmation against this are inclined to perceive transcendence as the Verb in which we participate—live, move, and have our being.

This Verb—the Verb of Verbs—is intransitive. It need not be conceived as having an object that limits its dynamism. That which it is over against is nonbeing. Women in the process of liberation are enabled to perceive this because our liberation consists in refusing to be "the Other" and asserting instead "I am"—without making another "the Other." Unlike Sartre's "us versus a third" (the closest approximation to love possible in his world), the new sisterhood is saying "us versus nonbeing." When Sartre wrote that "man [sic] fundamentally *is* the desire to be God," he was saying that the most radical passion of human life is to be a God who does not and cannot exist. The ontological hope of which I am speaking is neither this self-defication nor the simplistic reified images often lurking behind such terms as "Creator," "Lord," "Judge," that Sartre rightly rejects. It transcends these because its experiential basis is courageous *participation* in being. . . . It enables us to break out of this prison of subjectivity because it implies commitment together. . . .

The unfolding of God, then, is an event in which women participate as we participate in our own revolution. The process involves the creation of new space, in which women are free to become who we are, in which there are real and significant alternatives to the prefabricated identities provided within the enclosed spaces of patriarchal institutions. As opposed to the foreclosed identity allotted to us within those

---

Mary Daly

spaces, there is a diffused identity—an open road to discovery of the self and of each other.

The new space is located always "on the boundary." Its center is on the boundary of patriarchal institutions, such as churches, universities, national and international politics, families. Its center is the lives of women whose experience of becoming changes the very meaning of center for us by putting it on the boundary of all that has been considered central. . . .

The new space, then, has a kind of invisibility to those who have not entered it. It is therefore inviolable. At the same time it communicates power which, paradoxically, is experienced both as power of presence and power of absence. It is not political power in the usual sense but rather a flow of healing energy which is participation in the power of being. For women who are becoming conscious, that participation is made possible initially by casting off the role of "the Other" which is the nothingness imposed by a sexist world. The burst of anger and creativity made possible in the presence of one's sisters is an experience of becoming whole, of overcoming the division within the self that makes nothingness block the dynamism of being. Instead of settling for being a warped half of a person, which is equivalent to a self-destructive non-person, the emerging woman is casting off role definitions and moving toward androgynous being. This is not a mere "becoming equal to men in a man's world"—which would mean settling for footing within the patriarchal space. It is, rather, something like God speaking forth God-self in the new identity of women. While life in the new space may be "dangerous" in that it means living without the securities offered by the patriarchal system for docility to its rules, it offers a deeper security that can absorb the risks that such living demands. This safety is participation in *being,* as opposed to inauthenticity, alienation, non-identity—in a word, nonbeing.

The power of presence that is experienced by those who have begun to live in the new space radiates outward, attracting others. For those who are fixated upon patriarchal space it apparently is threatening. Indeed this sense of threat is fre-

---

quently expressed. For those who are thus threatened, the presence of women to each other is experienced as an absence. Such women are no longer empty receptacles to be used as "the Other," and are no longer internalizing the projections that cut off the flow of being. Men who need such projection screens experience the power of absence of such "objects" and are thrown into the situation of perceiving nothingness. . . .

Women's confrontation with the experience of nothingness invites men to confront it also. Many of course respond with hostility. The hostility may be open or, in some cases, partially disguised both from the men who are exercising it and from the women to whom it is directed. When disguised, it often takes seductive forms, such as invitations to "dialogue" under conditions psychologically loaded against the woman, or invitations to a quick and easy "reconciliation" without taking seriously the problems raised. Other men react with disguised hostility in the form of being "the feminist's friend," not in the sense of really hearing women but as paternalistic supervisors, analysts, or "spokesmen" for the Movement. Despite many avenues of nonauthentic response to the threat of women's power of absence, some men do accept the invitation to confront the experience of nothingness that offers itself when "the Other" ceases to be "the Other" and stands back to say "I am." In so doing men begin to liberate themselves toward wholeness, toward androgynous being. This new participation in the power of being becomes possible for men when women move into the new space.

Entry into the new space whose center is on the boundary of the institutions of patriarchy also involves entry into new time. To be caught up in these institutions is to be living in time past. . . . By contrast, when women live on the boundary, we are vividly aware of living in time present/future. Participation in the unfolding of God means also this time breakthrough, which is a continuing (but not ritually "repeated") process. The center of the new time is on the boundary of patriarchal time. What it is, in fact, is women's *own* time. It is our *life-time*. It is whenever we are living out of our own sense of reality, refusing to be possessed, conquered, and alienated by

---

the linear, measured-out, quantitative time of the patriarchal system. Women, in becoming who we are, are living in a qualitative, organic time that escapes the measurements of the system. For example, women who sit in institutional committee meetings without surrendering to the purposes and goals set forth by the male-dominated structure, are literally working on our own time while perhaps appearing to be working "on company time." The center of our activities is organic, in such a way that events are more significant than clocks. This boundary living is a way of being in and out of "the system." It entails a refusal of false clarity. Essentially it is being alive now, which in its deepest dimension is participation in the unfolding of God.